THE PRIMARY SUBJECT MANAGER'S HAND

The primary coordinator and OFSTED re-inspection

THE SUBJECT LEADER'S HANDBOOKS

Series Editor: Mike Harrison, Centre for Primary Education, School of Education, The University of Manchester, Oxford Road, Manchester, M13 9DP

The primary coordinator and OFSTED re-inspection

Phil Gadsby and Mike Harrison

FALMER PRESS
Taylor & Francis Group

UK   Falmer Press, 1 Gunpowder Square, London, EC4A 3DE

USA   Falmer Press, Taylor & Francis Inc., 325 Chestnut Street, 8th Floor, Philadelphia, PA 19106

First published in 1999

A catalogue record for this book is available from the British Library

ISBN 0 7507 0699 6 paper

Library of Congress Cataloging-in-Publication Data are available on request

Jacket design by Carla Turchini

Typeset in 10/14pt Melior and printed by Graphicraft Limited, Hong Kong

Contents

Part one
Your role as subject coordinator

Part two
How the inspection process works

Part three
Developing quality in your subject

Part four
Monitoring your subject or area

List of figures

Series editor's preface

This book has been prepared for primary teachers charged with the responsibility of acting as coordinators for various subject areas within their schools. It forms part of a series of new publications that set out to advise such teachers on the complex issues of improving teaching and learning through managing each element of the primary school curriculum.

Why is there a need for such a series? Most authorities recognise, after all, that the quality of primary children's work and learning depends upon the skills of their class teacher, not in the structure of management systems, policy documents or the titles and job descriptions of staff. Many today recognise that school improvement equates directly to the improvement of teaching, so surely all tasks, other than imparting subject knowledge, are merely a distraction for the committed primary teacher.

Nothing should take teachers away from their most important role, that is, serving the best interests of the class of children in their care and this book, and the others in the series, does not wish to diminish that mission. However, the increasing complexity of the primary curriculum and society's expanding expectations, make it very difficult for the class teacher to keep up to date with every development. Within traditional subject areas there has been an explosion of knowledge and new fields introduced such as science, technology, design, problem solving and health education, not to mention the uses of computers. These are now considered entitlements for primary children. Furthermore, we now expect all children to succeed at these studies, not just the fortunate few. All this has overwhelmed a class teacher system largely unchanged since the inception of primary schools.

Primary class teachers cannot possibly be an expert in every aspect of the curriculum they are required to teach. To whom can they turn for help? It is unrealistic to assume that such support will be available from the headteacher whose responsibilities have grown ever wider since the 1988 Educational Reform Act. Constraints, including additional staff costs, and the loss of benefits from the strength and security of the class teacher system, militate against wholesale adoption of specialist or semi-specialist teaching. Help therefore has to come from exploiting the talents of teachers themselves, in a process of mutual support. Hence primary schools have chosen many and varied systems of consultancy or subject coordination which best suit the needs of their children and the current expertise of the staff.

In fact, curriculum leadership functions in primary schools have increasingly been shared with class teachers through the policy of curriculum coordination for the past twenty years, especially to improve the consistency of work in language and mathematics. Since then each school has developed their own system and the series recognises that the one each reader is part of will be a compromise between the ideal and the possible. Campbell and Neill (1994) show that by 1991 nearly nine out of every ten primary class teachers had such responsibility and the average number of subjects each was between 1.5 and 2.2 (depending on the size of school).

These are the people for whom this series sets out to help to do this part of their work. The books each deal with specific issues whilst at the same time providing an overview of general themes in the management of the subject curriculum. The term *subject leader* is used in an inclusive sense and combines the two major roles that such teachers play when they have responsibility for subjects and aspects of the primary curriculum.

The subject focused books each deal with:

- *coordination* — a role which emphasises harmonising, bringing together, making links, establishing routines and common practice; and
- *subject leadership* — a role which emphasises providing information, offering expertise and direction, guiding the development of the subject, and raising standards.

Other books within the series give guidance on aspects of the curriculum of particular importance to coordinators such as assessment, special needs and coordination in small schools as well as this book which deals particularly with preparation for OFSTED re-inspection.

The purpose of the series is to give practical guidance and support to teachers; in particular, what to do and how to do it. They each offer help on the production, development and review of policies and schemes of work; the organisation of resources, and developing strategies for improving the management of the subject curriculum.

Each book in the series contains material that subject managers will welcome and find useful in developing their subject expertise and in tackling problems of enthusing and motivating staff.

Although written primarily for teachers who are subject coordinators, this book offers practical guidance and many ideas for anyone in the school who has a responsibility for the curriculum including teachers with an overall role in coordinating the whole or key stage curriculum and the deputy head and the headteacher.

In making the book easily readable we have drawn upon our considerable experience as primary teachers and headteachers, as OFSTED inspectors and as consultants and advisers to coordinators and others in school faced with re-inspection. The book is not a short-cut on *how to pass* but encourages readers to use the OFSTED framework in order to improve teaching and learning such that any outside observer can be informed, using a common language, about the progress the school has made.

Mike Harrison, Series Editor
May 1998

Introduction

In each of the books in this series authors have examined
ways in which coordinators can audit the quality of current
teaching and learning in their own schools. The major external
evaluation of primary schools is that carried out by the Office
for Standards in Education (OFSTED), and their inspections
are the focus of this book.

By now, all primary schools will have experienced their first
OFSTED inspection, but many individual teachers new to the
profession, and several who changed schools at just the 'right'
time, will not. This book is intended to assist those of you
preparing for such an inspection and to give you and your
colleagues an indication of the increased expectations implicit
in subsequent rounds of the inspection programme. By
understanding the processes involved, coordinators will
improve their own ability to examine the state of their subjects
and will be better prepared for the visit.

Section 9 (now 10) of the Education (Schools) Act 1992
requires all maintained primary schools to be inspected by Her
Majesty's Chief Inspector (HMCI), working from the Office for
Standards in Education. The act specifies that over a four year
cycle (now increased to six years) schools will be inspected in
order to identify their strengths and weaknesses, so helping
them to improve the quality of the education they provide for
pupils and thereby raise the standards achieved.

Between 1994 and 1998 all primary schools in England and Wales have been inspected and their performance reported upon under the provisions of either Section 9 of the Education (Schools) Act 1992 or Section 10 of The Schools Inspections Act 1996. Denominational voluntary aided schools had their religious education and collective worship separately inspected and reported on under Section 10 of the 1992 or Section 23 of the 1996 Act. From September 1998 all primary schools are being re-inspected within six years of their previous inspection.

The inspection of your school will examine the achievements and progress made by children in both key stages, their attitudes, the quality of the teaching they receive, the management and leadership provided, the accommodation and resources available, and the effectiveness of the use made of those resources, alongside issues of equal opportunities and special educational needs. Not all of the judgments made about each of these features will appear in the report but they will be submitted to OFSTED in the subject profile, which is the evidence base for the report.

The inspection is carried out by Her Majesty's Chief Inspector of Schools (HMCI) working from the Office for Standards in Education. It is carried out to statutory criteria, specified in the OFSTED *Framework for the Inspection of Schools*. The purpose of the inspection is to identify a school's strengths and weaknesses, so helping it to make plans to improve the quality of education it provides for its pupils and to raise the educational standards they achieve,

Inspectors are required to report upon the quality of education provided by the school; the educational standards achieved in the school; the extent to which the financial and other resources made available to the school are managed efficiently; and the spiritual, moral, social and cultural development of pupils at the school. The inspectors have to identify a clear agenda for action by the school's appropriate authority, usually its governing body. A summary of the report on the school is sent to all parents, to whom a copy of the full report must be made available if required. The appropriate authority has to respond with a plan of action to address the key issues raised by the inspection.

The inspection framework is detailed and comprehensive. The role of the subject coordinator in the inspection process reflects the way in which its importance has grown in recent years. The coordinator is increasingly regarded as central to the whole school's approach to managing the curriculum.

The purpose of this handbook is to support subject coordinators in primary schools in preparing for and undergoing the inspection. It provides the means for schools and their coordinators to identify and codify the role generally as a basis from which to make specific preparation for the inspection process. It considers the role of the coordinator in the context of how it has developed generally. It enables coordinators to relate these general requirements to the specific structures for curriculum management in his or her own school. It makes clear what the inspection framework will require of coordinators and how these expectations might be met.

The book will also be of interest to headteachers of primary schools in their role as overall curriculum managers.

Part one Your role as subject coordinator

Chapter 1

The development of the role and the inspection framework

> ❝ *A great deal of enthusiasm and expertise in specific curriculum areas has been locked into individual classrooms. It is only when we share knowledge and skills that the true potential of the professional teacher is realised.*   Harrison and Theaker (1989)

If you look at actual OFSTED inspection reports, which are now freely available and published via the Internet, you can gain a flavour of what the inspection process is about as far as subject reports are concerned. The following extract from a report shows you what you would be hoping to achieve for your subject or area of responsibility.

Leadership of the subject (science) is good. There is an effective whole school policy that was developed in collaboration with the rest of the staff. A well-structured long-term plan provides a framework for class teachers' mid- and short-term planning. The curriculum fully meets the statutory requirements. There are regular meetings with staff from the secondary school receiving the majority of pupils. Staff from the feeder infant school are also consulted. This ensures effective planning for progression across the key stages. Long-term planning is done by the coordinator and discussed with staff at curriculum meetings. The coordinator organises and contributes to staff development activities although there is no opportunity for the coordinator to work alongside other members of staff.

Extract from OFSTED report: junior school, 1996

By contrast, you would not like to receive the following:

> This subject (English) is insufficiently managed or monitored to
> support teaching, raise standards and identify resource needs.
>
> Large primary school, 1997

We can see that the role of the subject coordinator has come to
be regarded as central to the development and management of
the curriculum and how it is taught; to the realisation of the
school's aims and policies; to the quality of the pupils'
learning and the standards they achieve.

The development of the role

The role of the subject coordinator in the primary school
has not, of course, been invented by OFSTED. It has been a
significant focus in education policy for some years. Back in
1978 the primary survey *Primary Education in England:
A Survey by HM Inspectors of Schools* (DES, 1978) carried
out by Her Majesty's Inspectors (HMI) and published by the
Department for Education and Science (DES) was saying:

❝ *Effectiveness can be considerably enhanced if individual
teachers are given responsibility within the school for both the
planning and oversight of the work in relation to particular
aspects of the curriculum.* (paragraph 4.1)

The report was clear and specific about the kinds of things
these holders of posts of special responsibility might do:

❝ *It is important that teachers with special responsibility for say,
mathematics, should in consultation with the head, other
members of staff and teachers in neighbouring schools, draw
up schemes of work to be implemented in the school; give
guidance and support to other members of staff; assist in
teaching mathematics to other classes when necessary; and be
responsible for the procurement, within the funds made available, of the resources necessary for teaching the subject. They
should develop acceptable means of assessing the effectiveness*

> *of the guidance and the resources they provide, and this may involve visiting other classes in the school to see the work in progress.* (paragraph 8.46)

More recently *Primary Matters: A Discussion on Teaching and Learning in Primary Schools*, (OFSTED, 1994a) concentrated again on the subject coordinator:

> ❛ *Teachers who are subject managers for the whole school ('coordinator' is too limited a description) can be expected (a) to develop a clear view of the nature of their subject and its contribution to the wider curriculum of the school; (b) to provide advice and documentation to help teachers to teach the subject and interrelate its constituent elements; and (c) to play a major part in organising the teaching and the resources of the subject so statutory requirements can be covered.* (p. 9)

Subject coordinators (or subject managers in the terminology of *Primary Matters*) are seen as assuming delegated responsibility for subject management from the headteacher, (who has overall responsibility for managing the curriculum), which involves three clear strands: coordination, monitoring and evaluation. It is worth quoting the full list of responsibilities for each strand. Where a school has delegated subject management, each coordinator has coordination, monitoring and evaluation roles to some extent.

Coordination

- developing between the teaching team an agreed view of what constitutes the school curriculum and its relationship to the National Curriculum;
- identifying principles and procedures for interrelating the constituent parts of the curriculum;
- setting out principles and procedures for making and implementing curriculum decisions;
- establishing the roles and responsibilities of all those involved in curriculum decision making;
- organising the curriculum to help achieve the aims of the school; provide coverage of the statutory curriculum; and, hence promote the educational achievement of pupils.

Monitoring

- monitoring colleagues' planning and preparation to ensure appropriate coverage of the Attainment Targets and Programmes of Study of the statutory curriculum and to ensure coverage of the other aspects of the school's agreed curriculum;
- monitoring the work undertaken in classes to see how the work planned and prepared is actually taught and assessed.

Evaluation

Using the *OFSTED Framework for Inspection (OFSTED, 1994a), and School Evaluation Matters*, (OFSTED, 1998) and other sources to:

- evaluate the whole curriculum using the criteria of breadth, balance, continuity, progression, coherence and compliance with National Curriculum requirements;
- evaluate the teaching techniques and organisational strategies employed by colleagues and yourself, using the criterion of fitness for purpose;
- evaluating the standards and progress achieved by individuals and groups of children and looking for trends and patterns of achievement;
- evaluating the overall quality of education provided, including extra-curricular activities;
- 'evaluating the standards achieved and the quality of education provided'. (OFSTED, 1994a p. 8)

The Teacher Training Agency (TTA) has also made clear, in the promotion of agreed expectations for subject leaders what the core purposes of the role should be. The evidence from OFSTED inspections has shown that pupil achievement is higher when the role of the subject leader is clearly identified and effectively implemented. It is clear that effective subject leaders make a major contribution to improving schools and to raising the levels of pupil achievement. Thus the TTA (1997) in its *National Standards for Subject Leaders* sees their core functions as:

 ■ *To secure continuous improvement in the teaching of the subject in the school, producing the highest standards of*

pupil achievement and ensuring that all pupils develop their knowledge, understanding, skills and abilities within a secure, challenging and motivating educational environment.

■ *Within the context of the school and its policies, subject leaders are responsible for establishing and ensuring high standards of teaching and learning in their subject. They play a key role in monitoring, supporting and motivating other teachers and in setting targets for professional development and improvement, playing a major role by contributing to policy development at subject and school level and by evaluating impact on teaching and learning.*

■ *It is assumed that subject leaders work within a school-wide context. Subject leaders must be able to identify needs within their own subject and also recognise that these needs must be weighed against the overall needs of the school. It is vital that subject leaders have an understanding of how their subject contributes to the overall education and achievement of pupils.*

■ *Subject leaders play a key role in monitoring and evaluating pupil achievements. They use data and information to develop plans which aim to improve and sustain pupil achievement, motivation and discipline. These can be identified through the use of national and local benchmarks and through 'value added' measures and comparisons. Pupil achievement across a wide range of activities will be monitored.* (p. 9)

The achievement of these core purposes will be through the following key areas:
■ teaching, learning and the curriculum;
■ monitoring, evaluating and improving;
■ people and relationships;
■ managing resources;
■ accountability;
■ professional knowledge and understanding;
■ skills and abilities.

All of these key areas are dealt with in this handbook.

The quotes included so far will leave you in no doubt that the coordination of the curriculum and monitoring of standards and progress resulting from it are regarded as being at the heart of primary school management. That this should be so is entirely appropriate if you regard the core purpose of your school as the achievement of the highest possible standards of achievement for all of your children. The precise responsibility between the different people involved, for example the relationship between the particular responsibilities of the headteacher, and what subject coordinators do, will not be identical in each school. The particular balance between roles in any school will depend upon a number of factors. Some of these are explored in Chapter 2, which helps you to look at your role in your school. What we need to do now is consider the ways in which the development of expectations of the role of the coordinator have been incorporated into OFSTED's inspection process.

Primary school subject specialists raise standards

The use of primary school teachers with subject expertise has a highly positive impact on standards, says an Office for Standards in Education (OFSTED) report out today. But even the very best schools rarely use this expertise to its full potential.

The report, *The use of subject expertise to promote high standards at Key Stage 2: an illustrative survey*, is the result of visits by Her Majesty's Inspectors (HMI) to 70, mainly primary, schools in England. The schools' inspection reports showed that good use of subject expertise was an important factor contributing to high standards.

The report says that in primary schools, the traditional 'one teacher, one class' organisation has placed a heavy demand on the class teacher who has to meet far wider curricular requirements than subject teachers in secondary schools. Primary schools, however, have access to considerable professional expertise. Teachers are increasingly well qualified and often have extensive knowledge of at least one subject from their initial training. Nonetheless, the organisation of primary schools tends to restrict the possibility of teachers with subject expertise using their specialist knowledge outside their own classroom for the benefit of the entire school.

Among its main findings, the report says that:

■ successful schools are willing to move away from the 'one class, one teacher' model;

■ subject specialists have a positive influence on the quality of the teaching of non-specialists;

■ features of the best teaching by specialists are a confident command of the subject, a brisk pace to lessons and unusually high expectations which are invariably met by the pupils.

The report says that many of the schools in the study are good or very good, and several of them are outstanding. But even in those schools the available subject expertise is rarely used to its full potential much to the frustration of the school and the teachers concerned. In some schools imaginative ways are found to use the expertise productively and these form the case studies included in the report.

Some schools are more successful than others in using specialist knowledge. No single blueprint emerges from the survey. It does, however, describe and evaluate practice and show the difficulties and restraints faced by those schools which make an effort to raise standards by working from the subject strengths of their teachers.

The report advises caution in investing too much time and expertise in one subject to the detriment of others and, over-reliance on one teacher who may leave, with a resultant fall in the quality of work in the subject.

Extract from OFSTED press release 24 November 1997

The coordinator's role and the inspection schedule

When schools are inspected for a second or subsequent time, inspectors must also report on what has happened since the previous inspection. Full details of re-inspection regulations are set out in *Inspection and Re-inspection of Schools from September 1997: New Requirement and Guidance on their Implementation* (OFSTED, 1997). There is a section on school improvement in the inspection report. This consists of an analysis of how the school has improved since its earlier inspection. The starting point will be the findings of the previous inspection as detailed in the report and in particular its response to the key issues for action identified within it. Changes and progress considered to be most significant are those to do with standards of attainment. In evaluating and

Expectations of curriculum management and the roles and relationships of the various people involved in it are brought together in the OFSTED inspection schedule and guidance handbook: *Guidance on the Inspection of Nursery and Primary Schools* (OFSTED, 1995) Section 6.1 of the inspection schedule, concerned with leadership and management, requires inspectors to evaluate and report upon how well the governors of the school, headteacher and staff with management responsibilities contribute to the quality of the education provided by the school and the standards achieved by all of its pupils. They must report on the extent to which the school complies with statutory requirements, which of course include teaching of the programmes of Study of the National Curriculum.

reporting on these trends in attainment over time, inspectors will consider how well targets set or adopted by the school are being met. All schools have had to set their own improvement targets since September 1998, and inspectors will be keen to consider any means by which the school has monitored and evaluated its own progress towards reaching its targets. Target-setting is dealt with in more detail later in Chapter 9 of this handbook. When assessing the progress made by a school, inspectors will be interested in the previous and current levels of performance of pupils in the school, although they will have to balance these against possible contributory factors like changes in the socio-economic context of the school and the attainment of pupils on entry to the school.

There are clearly implications here for you as a subject coordinator. You will need to be aware of the findings of the previous inspection about your subject or area of responsibility and what the report actually says. This will be particularly important if your area has been specifically identified in the main findings or key issues for action of the earlier report. You will also need to be fully aware of and involved in your school's target-setting process, again particularly if your subject is targeted. You will have to have a view of progress in your subject over time, all issues which are picked up on again in Part 4 of the handbook.

In coming to their judgments, inspectors have to consider the extent to which:
■ strong leadership provides clear educational direction for the work of the school;
■ teaching and curriculum developments are monitored, evaluated and supported;
■ the school has aims, values and policies which are reflected through all of its work;
■ the school, through its development planning, identifies relevant priorities and targets, takes the necessary action and monitors and evaluates its progress towards achieving them;
■ there is a positive ethos in the school, which reflects its commitment to high achievements, an effective learning environment, good relationships and equality of opportunity for all pupils; and,
■ that all statutory requirements are met.

The inspection handbook is very clear that the headteacher is the professional leader of the school, responsible for the direction of its work and for its day to day management and organisation.

> *The headteacher is seen very much as the whole-school cur-*
> *riculum leader coordinating or orchestrating staffing, resources*
> *and time so as to give all pupils full access to the curriculum . . .*
>
> (Richards, 1995)

In an effective school the headteacher has direct concern for the sustained improvement of quality and standards, for equality of opportunity for all pupils and for the development of policies and the use of resources to reach its stated goals. However, the handbook also makes it clear that other staff, 'such as coordinators', have leadership and management functions, where they hold responsibility for aspects of the school's curriculum and organisation. Thus in a well-managed school such responsibilities are clearly defined and there is effective delegation, as it is clear that headteachers have insufficient time for direct management of the subject curriculum themselves (Blease and Lever, 1992). Staff should understand the role they play in the development and running of the school.

The responsibility of coordinators is related in particular to the inspection criteria concerned with the monitoring, evaluation and support of the curriculum and how it is taught. This criterion applies to all staff with management responsibility. It emphasises that a test of effective leadership and management is a commitment to monitoring and evaluating teaching and curriculum and taking action to sustain and improve their quality. This is very much in line with the focus of the inspection process on what are clearly and rightly seen as the core functions of the school. It is about teaching and learning of the curriculum, about how management focuses on and facilitates the achievement of quality provision in this core function and how, ultimately, everything will be judged in terms of the standards the pupils achieve and the progress they make in their learning. There is no doubt that the inspection schedule is to a large extent outcome driven. The outcomes are the educational standards achieved by the pupils in their academic attainment and progress; their attitudes, behaviour and personal development and their attendance at school. The input, or contributory factors, which lead to the outcomes found are the curriculum provided by the school; how progress through it by pupils is assessed; the school's provision for pupil's spiritual, moral, social and cultural development; the support and guidance given to pupils to achieve their overall welfare and how partnership with parents and the community contributes to the standards achieved. The most important input element, however, is the quality of the teaching which is responsible for providing the other elements. The leadership and management of the school, the staffing, accommodation and resources it provides and its overall efficiency in using the resources made available to it to achieve quality provision and high standards are other significant factors.

What has emerged is a system of curriculum management centred on the prime responsibility of the headteacher as the leading professional in the school but supported by all staff with curriculum management responsibility. Through effective systems of coordination, monitoring, evaluation and support there should be an impact in terms of enhancing the quality of educational provision and the standards achieved by the pupils. The system should be part of a whole school structure of roles and responsibilities that is understood and adhered to by everyone involved.

Evidence for the effectiveness of curriculum leadership and management in the school will be collected primarily through subject inspection. In primary school inspections, inspectors must complete a standard subject profile for each of the core National Curriculum subjects of English, mathematics and science. Most contractors also require inspectors to contribute to the overall evidence base by completing them for all subjects. A summary of the subject profile is reproduced in Figure 1.1.

Although it is only mandatory for the core subjects, as a guide to the elements involved in achieving quality it is of value to you if you are a non-core subject coordinator, as the nature of your task is clarified. It is the summation and analysis of

FIG 1.1
Summary of the subject profile

The subject profile

Attainment and progress:
> evidence of attainment in relation to national standards or expectations; evidence of pupils' progress in relation to prior attainment.

Attitudes, behaviour and personal development:
> evidence of pupils' attitudes to learning in the subject, behaviour, quality of relationships and other aspects of personal development.

Teaching:
> evidence of the strengths and weaknesses in the teaching of the subject.

The curriculum and assessment:
> evidence of strengths and weaknesses of curriculum planning in the subject; and of procedures for and accuracy of assessing pupils' progress in the subject.

Pupils' spiritual, moral, social and cultural development:
> summary of evidence and findings of the subject's contribution to the provision for pupils' spiritual, moral, social and cultural development.

Leadership and management:
> evidence of how well leadership, management and coordination of the subject contribute to the quality of the provision and then educational standards achieved.

Staffing, accommodation and learning resources:
> evidence of the quality of staffing, accommodation and resources and the effects of any good or poor provision on the quality of education and the educational standards achieved in the subject.

Efficiency:
> summary of evidence and findings as to how efficiently and effectively the resources made available for the subject are managed and deployed.

---

evidence from each aspect for each subject inspected that will form the basis for overall judgments on the school. As you can see, the performance in individual subjects is thus critical to the way in which the school as a whole is seen.

The evidence of the inspectors' judgments about your subject will come from a number of sources. Direct observation of the teaching and learning going on in the school is the major focus. This will be supplemented by the inspection of the work the pupils produce, discussion with pupils about their work, by the examination of any documentation — policies, guidelines, schemes of work — which support teaching and learning in your subject, by looking at assessment and test results where these are available and by a more or less formal discussion or interview with you about your subject in your school and how it is managed. Each of these elements of the inspection is dealt with in detail in Part 2 of the book, to help you to be as well-prepared as possible for the inspection process. It goes without saying, of course, that the best and most effective preparation for inspection is to do the job as well as you can over a period of time. This handbook is aimed at helping you to do just that.

Your role as coordinator, therefore, will be regarded to a significant extent as a management and leadership one. It isn't just about your own teaching performance. Nor is it just about your analysis. Being a coordinator is action-centred. The many changes and increased demand on the time of all involved in education currently means that

> *managers and leaders have less time and inclination to gather data, analyse it and form conceptual generalisations from which to plan strategies for action, [in the course of their management activity.]*
>   (Kelly, 1995)

Get on with it! You will be expected to be clear about your responsibilities and how you carry them out and to be fully informed of the current position of your subject in relation to curriculum management in the school overall. In the next chapter we begin to consider how you will need to be clear about the role you fulfil in your particular school. This will then lead on to the ways in which you can enhance the quality of your subject in a way that not only meets the requirements of OFSTED but the educational needs of your pupils.

Chapter 2

Your role in your school

> ❝ *The management of the curriculum, may be regarded as being almost identical with the management of the school itself . . . The curriculum remains the centrepiece of school life and its management . . . the main preoccupation of the staff.*
>
> Alan and Audrey Paisley (1989)

We have seen how the role of the subject coordinator and the expectations of the role have developed and how they have been incorporated into the OFSTED inspection process. It is important that as a subject coordinator you are able to define clearly what are the actions and activities necessary to fulfil your role and responsibilities. You should be aware, also, of the constraints and difficulties that could hamper your carrying them out and how these might be overcome.

Range of tasks

The potential range of tasks for coordinators is enormous. The following list is constructed from actual jobs that coordinators have done or been expected to do in a variety of schools. They are in no hierarchy of importance.

Many coordinators are expected:
- to attend inservice training (INSET) for personal expertise and development and to feed back to colleagues;

- to attend liaison, cluster-group meetings with other schools, which may be cross-phase, to share developments, ideas and to feed back to own staff;
- to engage in personal reading and research to enhance their own expertise in order to support and develop colleagues' skills and understandings;
- to set high standards in their own class/teaching which can be used as a guide to expectations and a model for good practice in the subject;
- to lead staff in the development of policy and schemes of work, which could include devising, drafting, leading meetings and discussions in working parties, re-drafting, finalising and publishing;
- to audit resource needs for policy implementation and provide resources within the school's policy and procedures for resource allocation;
- to provide help and guidance to colleagues in planning their children's work;
- to coordinate displays in the school which promote and enhance the subject for which they are responsible;
- to report to senior management and governors as and when required to keep them informed of all issues relating to their subject;
- to teach directly or assist in the teaching of their subject;
- to observe colleagues teaching the subject;
- to lead assessment agreement trials/moderation meetings in the subject;
- to review and comment upon colleagues' curriculum planning in the subject;
- to evaluate children's work in the subject;
- to administer and analyse tests and assessments within the subject;
- to engage in formal conversations and discussions with children, colleagues, parents, HMI, Local Education Authority (LEA) advisers and advisory teachers, consultants about the subject and how it is taught;
- to analyse and use the outcomes of formal external reviews of their school's performance in the subject, for example LEA review, OFSTED inspection;
- to contribute to the school development plan;
- to monitor the reflection within their subject of cross-curricular issues such as equal opportunities; special

educational needs; assessment; multi-cultural education and personal and social education, where these are relevant.

As you can see, the potential list is huge and exhaustive, not to say exhausting. But you will not be expected to fulfil all of these duties nor should you be expected to attempt the majority unless the appropriate support and whole-school structures are in place.

Bell (1992) looked at the most common jobs carried out by primary coordinators and showed that there was a high correlation between ten key tasks, shown here in their rank order.
1 Communicating with the headteacher
2 Exercising curricular leadership
3 Communicating with staff
4 Organising resources
5 Establishing and maintaining continuity throughout the school.
6 Organising in-service courses
7 Liaising between head and staff
8 Establishing recording systems
9 Motivating staff
10 Engaging in curriculum development

Such a list of potential tasks might be classified under three broad headings: those concerned with development of your subject; those concerned with coordinating the subject and supporting colleagues as they teach it; those concerned with monitoring and evaluating the teaching and learning of the subject and the impact this is having on the standards children are achieving as a result; and, the progress that they are making in their learning of the subject.

It might be useful for you to construct a simple three column grid so that each activity can be inserted under what seems to be the most appropriate function. This will provide the basis for future consideration as you work through the ideas in the book which are targeted on improving your performance as subject coordinator. In order to carry out the activity on p. 22 it will be useful if you leave a space between each activity you record to enable notes to be made about the effectiveness with which you think you are operating and the reasons for the degree of effectiveness identified. As you read through the handbook and carry out further activities, you will be able to return to the grid, adding notes based on your completion of

Suggestion

Activity 1
From the list of activities that subject coordinators might be engaged in (and any that you might wish to add) identify those that you at present carry out. Attempt to classify them according to the categories suggested: developing quality; coordination and support; monitoring and evaluation.
Keep the list for later.

the tasks. Inevitably there is some overlap between the three functions but for the purposes of analysis and for a record of your development in understanding the role, it will be valuable. The example grid below gives some examples of the kind of thing which might be included.

Coordinator role analysis		
Curriculum development activities	**Support and coordination activities**	**Monitoring and evaluation activities**
Lead staff INSET on children writing poetry.	Informal talks with newly qualified teacher about the writing process.	Looking at writing displays in school to check the range and genres being used.
I need help in planning a good training day	*I am good at relating to staff on a one to one basis.*	*I am very clear about the writing requirements of the National Curriculum*

Possible constraints

We now turn to consider the possible constraints you may experience to the effective carrying out of any or all of your duties. Personal confidence may be one. This may be related to your real or self-perceived lack of expertise in your subject. It may be due to lack of experience, knowledge, skill, training or confidence in some of the personal qualities required to carry out your functions: in inter-personal skills; as a leader of meetings; as a writer of policy. Our next chapter concentrates on these in more detail and includes other activities for you to try.

Discussion may have helped to clarify functions and responsibilities of different members of staff within your area. Together you may usefully detail what each of your roles in this process will be. The chart below was originally constructed for IT coordinators to use in their schools to attempt to clarify the many facets of their own role and the responsibilities of others. You could well find that there are equivalent subject specific tasks in your area and you might well wish to use this as a model. Figure 2.1 has been modified from Clemson (1996).

The allocation of roles will depend on your school situation and there will be variations, but the discussion which leads

Allocation of roles and responsibilities in an effective school						
Task	SMT	Head	Coordinator	All staff	Contract out	Others
Organise and manage groups to write subject policy						
Alert others to local support services						
Assist in the design of subject development plans						
Responsible for ordering and distributing equipment and apparatus around the school						
Ensure equality of opportunity within the subject						
Identify needs and formulate policies for cross-curricular links						
Plan and provide subject INSET for other teachers						
Keep abreast of current philosophies in subject						
Alert others to the uses of subject as a tool to enhance learning in the subject						
Attend all the courses offered by the LEA						
Oversee and ensure the balanced delivery of all ATS in the subject curriculum						
Evaluate classroom practice in teaching the subject						
Inform other staff of good, bad and interesting practice in subject						
Keep a list of hardware and software available for teaching in subject						
Negotiate the purchase of site licences for key places of software needed to teach subject						
Recommend appropriate software for pupil and teacher needs						
Represent the school at LEA meetings for subject coordinators						
Liaise cross-phase to ensure continuity of teaching in the subject						
Deliver subject to all pupils in the school						
Keep records of pupils' progress through levels of attainment in subject						
Prepare reports on individual pupils' progress in subject						

adapted from Clemson (1996)

FIG 2.1
Role and responsibilities of subject coordinators

to decisions about such an allocation may well be to the advantage of you as coordinator. Many heads and other staff will not be aware of the complexities and sheer volume of the role. It might well lead to discussions of time allocation to match the extent of the tasks it is agreed that you should carry out. Working together to create or revise the policy document may offer a means of evaluation of the work being planned. How does it match up to your policy's ideals? It may also help new staff to settle in and reveal the role they play in the processes in your school. You might wish to ask recently arrived teachers whether any of the documents they were given helped them in their first terms? How did the policy fare by comparison with the others?

Relationships with colleagues might pose problems for a variety of reasons: relative status and/or experience; differences in values or personality. One of your authors remembers well the look of contempt on the face of the deputy head, who had spent forty years in the school, when, as the young and newly appointed coordinator for mathematics, he handed her a new scheme of work. An ostentatious sniff, the dropping of the document from a great height into her desk drawer and the finality of its noisy closure, before she continued with her task of writing long division sums on the blackboard, said it all. Never again would those hours of work see the light of day in her classroom!

Lack of time both generally and in relation to your other duties, such as your class or other coordinator roles, is clearly an issue for many coordinators. A lack of resources and the money to get them is another. It may be that there is over-expectation or a lack of support from senior management. And even where there is good will and the intention to support, a major constraint will be if there is a lack of any coherent whole-school approach to overall management of the curriculum and the definition of the roles of individuals.

There has been a growing recognition of the value of headteachers delegating curriculum responsibility in all subjects. Curriculum consultants, implying specialist expertise, have become curriculum coordinators, suggesting a managerial role.

Mike Harrison and Steve Gill, (1992) in their book *Primary School Management*, argue that the degree to which any particular primary school has developed such policies may be indicated by:

- the nature of the decisions curriculum coordinators feel confident in making without recourse to the headteacher;

- the understanding of the role shown by the person or persons to whom each coordinator is responsible and the mechanisms by which their work is monitored;

- the degree of consideration of personal needs and circumstances demonstrated in the choice and handling of coordinators;

- the strength of the structures of organisation which support coordinators (e.g. class release time, training);

- whether coordinators are respected as models of good practice in their specialist areas; (Does the headteacher act as a good working model for the relationships coordinators are encouraged to develop with other teachers?)

- the ways in which coordinators are enabled to learn personnel management skills from each other; and

- the degree to which coordinators work in harmony with the school's stated aims (see Activity 2).

In primary schools responsibility for the work of each individual class is effectively devolved to their class teacher. Whether this state of affairs leads to independence or interdependence will depend on both the school's management structure, the level of active management and the skills of the school's curriculum coordinators.

Expectations of staff may also use up both your time and goodwill. More than one IT coordinator has been urgently called from her classroom to reload paper into a colleague's printer or one, whom one of the authors met recently, was asked to come and switch a machine on because rain had

Suggestion

Activity 2
Consider each of these features and write down your opinion of the extent of the delegation of responsibility in your own school. How will this affect your role? ...

Suggestion

Activity 3
Refer to the grid you have constructed which indicates your coordinator duties under the three headings of quality development; coordination and support; monitoring and evaluation. Analyse each activity you have identified in terms of how well you think you may be achieving it. Decide upon the reasons why you are more or less effective in each area. Consider your answers to Activity 2 and now add notes of your views to the original grid.

been dripping into a computer overnight and 'it might be dangerous'. The coordinator wondered if this might be a measure of her popularity rating!

As a change agent in the school Schrag, Nelson and Siminowsky's (1985) six Cs of change may help you to become more effective:

Challenge	help staff perceive change as a challenge rather than a threat
Communicate	keep staff informed
Commitment	involve staff in diagnosis of the need for change, the planning, design and implementation of the change
Control	help staff feel that they are not powerless in the face change and through participation and involvement they will be able to influence the course of the change
Confidence	build confident, resilient staff who do not read any implications about their worth into the change
Connect	network with other individuals and organisations who are undergoing change to help staff to develop awareness of the inevitability of change and a more sophisticated approach to adapting to change.

Clearly, some of these constraints can be overcome by the individual more easily than others. It may be simpler to gain subject knowledge and expertise than to influence your senior management team, but what is important is that you try to be as objective as possible about the context within which you operate in your school. As a general rule you might think it more sensible to be fulfilling a relatively modest role fully and effectively than to be failing because the demands and expectations you have set yourself are unrealistically high in relation to the constraints you face.

As a result of completing Activities 1 to 3 you should be beginning to build up a picture of what you actually do currently as a coordinator, how well you feel that you are doing it and what are the main reasons for the current level of performance. What you should have is the beginning of a simple SWOT analysis — an identification of the strengths and weaknesses in your performance of the coordinator's role and the main threats to your level of effectiveness as well as an indication of where there may be opportunities for improvement.

Organising the coordinator's tasks

In order to control and keep track of the various strands of your role and the activities you undertake, it is useful to build up your own coordinator's file. Many subject leaders in primary schools now use them. The information is probably best kept in a loose-leaf file with dividers of some kind, so that it can be added to, modified and parts discarded as necessary. It will become both a management tool and a record of your work and achievement in carrying out your responsibilities. The following indicates the kinds of details you might wish to include:

- brief school and staff details;
- copy of parts of the school development plan relevant to your area;
- any school generic policies to do with roles and responsibilities;
- your job description;
- policies and schemes of work for your subject or area plus any general policies, such as assessment, equal opportunities, teaching and learning, health and safety, which are relevant;
- National Curriculum information for your subject;
- assessment information\data for your subject, including task and test results and results from other tests, such as standardised reading tests;
- action plans for your subject;
- evaluations of action taken;
- personal professional development plans and reviews;
- record of INSET attended, relevant INSET attended by colleagues and any evaluations, information;
- any in-house INSET activities you organise or deliver, with evaluations if appropriate;

- record\inventory of resources;
- a record of your monitoring and evaluation activities.

Don't worry if you have not got all of this! Review what you have, make sure that it is organised and start to target important gaps in a systematic way. This handbook will help you. Such a file when completed, and the actual contents will evolve in a way most useful to you, will be extremely helpful in preparing for and participating in any interviews or discussions with OFSTED inspectors.

Conclusion

Parts 3 and 4 of this book consist of detailed consideration of the elements of the coordinator role identified, giving ideas and suggestions as to how they might be effectively carried out. Part 2 examines how, during an OFSTED inspection, inspectors will attempt to judge the effectiveness of curriculum leadership and management and how you as coordinator can give them a clear picture of what you do as your part of the overall process. As already suggested you can use your analysis grid as a check list as you work through the remainder of the book. Opportunities to revisit and revise your position are given and your coordinator file can be built up as you work at your role and your performance in school.

Not everything will be possible. Your analysis has probably already demonstrated that. But you have begun to work out exactly what your role is and to document it. More will be said about documentation in Chapter 6. What you need to remember is that inspectors should not be making judgments about exactly what your role should be nor how it should be carried out. What they will be interested in is the extent to which what is actually achieved matches the aims and objectives of the role, which ultimately is about its focus on school improvement and the progress pupils are making in their learning. It will certainly be no good in an OFSTED inspection to have an unrealistic policy with declared processes not being implemented and stated objectives not being achieved. The secret is to have manageable short-term

FIG 2.2
Example of a job description

An example job description

A possible job description for the role of the curriculum coordinator as the basis for analysis and discussion:

- keep personally well-informed and up to date about the subject knowledge specific to your area of responsibility;
- prepare and keep under review a curriculum policy statement and scheme of work for the school in collaboration with the headteacher, staff, governors and other appropriate parties;
- provide guidance and support to staff in implementing policy and schemes of work, paying particular attention to the needs of newly qualified teachers, teachers new to the staff and supply teachers;
- arrange appropriate school and externally based INSET for staff and evaluate its usefulness and effectiveness.
- organise and be responsible for purchasing, with funds made available, the resources necessary for the subject, maintain an up to date inventory and check that members of staff are aware of how to use the resources;
- monitor and evaluate the effectiveness of work in the subject throughout the school, including the quality of teaching and learning and the progress and achievement of pupils;
- use monitoring information to set targets for improvement in your subject, taking account of any local and national comparative information;
- monitor the extent to which your subject contributes to the key skills of literacy, oracy, numeracy and information technology and to the pupils' spiritual, moral, social and cultural education and see that it provides equal opportunities for all pupils;
- assist with the diagnosis of pupils' learning difficulties and monitor the provision of your subject for pupils with special educational needs (SEN) through their individual education plans (IEPs), in collaboration with your special needs coordinator (SENCO);
- develop and maintain effective working liaisons with other schools, professionals and relevant agencies, with parents and with the local community where this is relevant;
- lead by example by fulfilling school policy to demonstrate high standards of teaching of your subject which sustain and raise pupils' motivation, behaviour and achievement;
- report, as required by school policy, to the headteacher, senior management team, governing body and parents on pupils' progress and the achievement of strategic plans for your subject or area;
- contribute, through your coordination responsibility, to the overall school development plan.

targets and a clear plan of action for achieving targets in good order, themes re-visited in Part 4.

You may already be aware that the achievement of your targets and success in your role will depend to a significant extent upon how you can influence colleagues to change what they do and how they do it. The final chapter of this first section recognises that your role as coordinator is moving you into the realms of middle management and that you will need to develop and use generic management skills if you are to operate effectively.

Ultimately, if everything is to be fully efficient, your coordinator role in your school should be clearly defined and known to all. This chapter concludes with an example job description (Figure 2.2).

This job description is by no means definitive and your own job description should have been arrived at through a process of negotiation and development so that it serves the needs of you and your own school. The detail of how the various elements in such a job description, which reflect the potential demands made of the role, can best be achieved are all contained in this book.

| Chapter 3 | The primary coordinator as middle manager |

As coordinator, OFSTED will recognise that you are carrying out a delegated responsibility on behalf of the headteacher. Have you established with him or her agreed terms of reference? Do you have a record of this? Try to understand how your responsibilities fit into the management structure of the school as a whole. Can you define the dividing line between a classteacher's autonomy and your responsibility to develop and implement a whole school plan? Make sure that you recognise the school's stated central purposes and aims in the work you do and any changes to improve teaching and learning you are trying to achieve.

The subsequent sections of the handbook concentrate in detail on the range of activities you will need to be involved in if you are to be successful in your coordinator role.

> ❝ *Coordinators are teachers who are subject managers for the whole school ('coordinator' is too limited a description).*
>
> (from *Primary Matters*, OFSTED, 1994a)

In order to complete these tasks you will, to some degree, require a set of skills and abilities that can be described as

---

To be an effective coordinator your first considerations must be amongst the following:

- How much do you know about the past and present situation and the opinions of the teachers with whom you will be working?
- How clear are you about the changes you want to see in the way your subject is considered, planned, organised, integrated with the rest of the curriculum?
- What will you be satisfied with?
- Are you willing to be fully committed to and involved with colleagues?
- Are you prepared to make the changes yourself?

management tools. It is beyond the scope of this book to analyse these in detail, but this chapter endeavours to raise your awareness of your role as middle manager, to indicate the range of skills and abilities that may be involved and to point you in the direction of how you may acquire, develop and use them.

As a coordinator you will be involved with the curriculum and the ways in which it is taught and learned, which is why inspectors will want to speak with you. Your monitoring and evaluation of the effectiveness of the structures and processes involved in the teaching and learning process will make strengths and weaknesses apparent to you. You will be involved with managing physical resources. The most important resource in your school, however, will be the people resources and in order to achieve your curriculum teaching and learning objectives you will be dealing, inevitably, with people and relationships. To become a successful coordinator you will need to develop professional knowledge and understanding and the skills and abilities within the area of management that will enable you to utilise them.

Taken as a whole, if your role is fully developed, OFSTED inspectors will acknowledge that you are carrying out an impressive array of core management functions including:

- curriculum development;
- professional and staff development;
- administration;
- managing people;
- managing resources;
- financial management;
- development planning;
- monitoring; and,
- evaluation.

For all of these functions, at various levels, you will need a range of management and leadership skills and understandings. This chapter cannot be exhaustive about them. There are a number of books available which you can read if you wish to go more deeply into the background. A good one is Neville West's *Middle Management in the Primary School: A Development Guide for Curriculum Leaders, Subject*

Managers and Senior Staff (1995). Subsequent sections of the handbook, however, will make implicit reference to the management functions identified.

> ❝ *Leadership for meaning, leadership for problem solving, collegial leadership, leadership as shared responsibility, leadership that serves school purposes, leadership that is tough enough to demand a great deal from everyone, and leadership that is tender enough to encourage the heart — these are the images of leadership we need for schools as communities.*　(Sergiovanni, 1996)

Whether the skills are predominantly management or leadership will depend upon your view of the tasks required to fulfil the role and the school's culture of coordinator activities. Whereas management focuses largely on the present and is dominated by issues of continuity and stability, leadership is:

- an art rather than a science;
- focused on policy rather than execution;
- concerned with values rather than facts;
- to do with generalism rather than specialism;
- the use of broad strategies rather than specific tactics;
- concerned with philosophy rather than action;
- reflective rather than active;
- concerned with human as opposed to material resources; and,
- focused on deliberation rather than detail.

(after Hodgkinson, 1991)

In order to be an effective leader one also needs to be an efficient manager. However, management skills are necessary but not sufficient for effective leadership.

Gaining expertise

Whatever your opinion, there are in common to both perspectives major areas in your personal development that you will need to consider. You will need to know, for example, how to acquire and maintain a high level of subject knowledge. As we have indicated earlier, you may well not be the natural expert within your school for the subject or area for which you have responsibility. How to gain expertise through reading and attending INSET are skills in themselves, in particular the ability to target and prioritise what will be of most value to you. The following list identifies some of the key sources of information which can help you to build on your knowledge and understanding of your subject:

- relevant research in books and articles;
- national inspection evidence;
- national and comparative test and assessment data;
- information and guidance from OFSTED, TTA, the Qualifications and Curriculum Authority (QCA) and similar national bodies;
- the work and publications of subject specific organisations such as the Association for Science Education (ASE), Association of the Teachers of Mathematics (ATM), Micros and Primary Education (MAPE);
- INSET courses provided by Local Education Authorities (LEAs); by college and university education departments and by the increasing number of private consultancy and training firms.

As coordinator for any subject you will need to be aware of particular statutory requirements within your subject and health and safety issues.

Gaining and keeping up to date with the nature of developments within your subject or area of responsibility is one thing, and as indicated requires careful organisation and time management. Effective management of time is in itself an important skill and one, which as a class teacher managing a class and classroom in a primary school, that you will be well aware of! We all have different ways of trying to make the best possible use of a resource that always seems to be in short supply. Remember, despite some similarities, time is not the same as money. With money you can spend it today or tomorrow and if you don't have enough you can borrow some and pay it back later. Time is a different commodity; you cannot have an hour of next week to spend today. The next few minutes are unique in your life. They will never return. The art of time management is to spend the day, hour, and minute to maximum effect. Much has been published on the issue of time management but the following are key elements:

- plan your time, don't just hope for the best; know what needs to be done and allocate time for it; try to prioritise

what is most important; as Drucker (1967) says in his book
— *The Effective Executive* — 'do first things first and
second things not at all,';

■ be clear and realistic in the targets you set yourself to
achieve, getting a limited amount done in the time available
is better than setting unrealistic challenges and facing the
demoralisation of not achieving them.

Work smarter not harder is the maxim. There is probably no
short cut to being an effective manager of time.

> ❝ *Efficiency can only begin when the nature of the job in hand
> has been clearly formulated and a determination to stick to it
> established.*   (Patrick Whitaker (1983) in *The Primary Head*)

The benefits of a smarter use of time are thought to be:
■ the satisfaction of getting things done on time;
■ no longer being driven by deadlines;
■ achieving better results and more quickly;
■ having goals and setting priorities;
■ not finding large jobs so daunting by breaking them down
into manageable chunks;
■ stopping doing too many things at once;
■ feeling in control of your own life;
■ able to go home with a clear conscience;
■ able to stop worrying;
■ not having to take work home so often;
■ relationships at work will improve;
■ relationships at home will improve;
■ my health will improve.

However, this is putting the cart before the horse. These are
not just the consequences of better use of time they are also the
prerequisites. What are the biggest time wasters?

Time wasters

Lack of objectives, priorities and planning

Good time management means getting full value for the time
we spend. This does not mean saving two or three minutes

> Planning is an unnatural activity. It is far more fun to **do** something. The nicest thing about **not** planning is that failure comes as a complete surprise rather than being preceded by a period of worry and depression.
>
> John Harvey-Jones

doing little jobs more effectively. It means looking at the day, the week, the month and making a plan which will get us to where we want to be in the available time. (See West-Burnham's (1997) *Managing Quality in Schools* for an analysis of whether the reality of your working life matches your job purpose. Without a plan we drift from task to task and get discouraged. We all have days when despite being very busy we feel 'nothing really got done today'.)

Frequently this is because we do not have real goals in mind. Successful coordinators find that they need long range objectives which are:

- **Measurable**

    so they can plot their progress;
- **Attainable**

    so they appear to everyone to be within reach;
- **Demanding**

    so that success will carry with it some satisfaction;
- **Consistent**

    both with the needs of the school and with your philosophy;
- **Flexible**

    so that alterations are possible if circumstances change; and,
- **Written**

    otherwise you will forget.

If the objectives and the means can be agreed with your colleagues (who will eventually implement the curriculum) so much the better. Having set such goals plans need to be drawn up to achieve them, otherwise crisis management will be the result.

Crisis management

Crisis management is fire fighting. Sometimes we spend so long recovering from previous mistakes that we have no time to prevent the next fire from starting and thus the cycle begins again. Pressured into a hasty decisions without deliberation or exploration of better alternatives we keep setting up disasters in the making. In our experience, when OFSTED come to school, teachers spend many hours from early morning to late in the evening preparing for the observations. Can they, with your help work smarter not harder?

Murphy's three laws are the chronology of a crisis.
1   Nothing is as simple as it seems.
2   Everything takes longer than you think (we set unrealistic deadlines).
3   If anything can go wrong — it will.

Lack of sound planning and insufficient monitoring of progress, which allows you to take corrective action, will allow Murphy to triumph. As will not taking account of changing priorities, information blockages, human error and mechanical breakdown.

When your goal is clear and tasks have been scheduled to attain it, then deadlines can be set with a cushion to take account of hiccups. We need a contingency plan to limit the damage if things do go wrong. But where no plan is laid and the disposal of time is left purely to chance chaos is sure to reign.

Interruptions

We like to think of ourselves as approachable and available to our colleagues but the *open door policy* scarcely ever leads to enhanced communication and consumes your time. A block of uninterrupted time is a precious commodity and needs to be guarded. You will need such time if you are to carry out the activities recommended in this book. You need time for reflection too.

Close your classroom door when the children have gone home. Open should mean accessible. Anyone needing information or a decision will still get it, eventually, but you will also get some peace. Insecure managers need to show their accessibility by allowing people to drop in at any time. This encourages overdependence and upward delegation of decisions, and leads to interruptions which cause fragmentation of the day and interfere with the achievement of your own objectives.

The major problem with the open door policy is the inflexibility and loss of freedom it implies. Responsiveness to changing situations, the varying needs of colleagues and the changing priorities of the job are the hallmarks of the good manager. All suggest the need for freedom to keep the door open or shut. The key is not the door. It is you and how you handle the situation.

Batch your interruptions. Make yourself available at set times such as before school on Tuesday and after school on Thursday. Encourage staff to come to see you then and to save their problems until those times. But be careful not to interrupt yourself!

The cluttered desk

We all have excuses for the state of our desks: 'I can find anything — in time'. So why is it so harmful? Well it does take time, and also time to find out what isn't there. What about when you are absent? No-one can do your work if they cannot find what is needed. But the worst feature is that you suffer interruptions every time you look at it.

Why do we do it?
The clutter consists of all the things we don't want to forget. This technique works so well that every time we see them we remember — and hence are interrupted in the thing we are working on. As the stacks grow higher we can't remember what's underneath. We spend time looking through the items to see if the things we didn't want to forget remind us to do things, which of course they do.

Solutions
1 Clear your desk of everything except the work in hand.
2 Do not permit other things to be put on your desk, by children, secretaries or the headteacher until you are ready for them.
3 Resist the temptation to leave the work you are doing for another possibly more appealing task.
4 Send the completed work on its way.
5 Have junk mail screened/listed.
6 Think about the effectiveness of your filing system. Remember 90 per cent of everything we keep we eventually throw away without looking at it again. The trick is to know which is the useful 10 per cent.

7 Delegate where you can. Paper follows responsibilities.
8 Keep a **to do** list.
9 Handle everything only once. Approve it, reject it, send for more information or throw it away.

The overload which leads to piles of paper, official documents and half-written reports is possibly because we should not have accepted so many jobs in the first place. So developing the means to off-load work to other colleagues might help us in a number of ways.

Failure to delegate

Management is achieving things through others. By definition, therefore, failure to delegate must mean failure to manage. Ask yourself 'How much of this could have been done by someone else?'

Reasons we give for not delegating some aspects of the work in hand include:
■ insecurity 'do it yourself syndrome';
■ lack of confidence in colleague;
■ being understaffed.

And several coordinators report failure when they have attempted delegation because of:
■ giving unclear or incomplete instructions;
■ failing to establish appropriate controls;
■ not delegating authority commensurate with responsibility.

However, when successful not only will you be relieved of a task but there will be enhanced motivation in the person you have trusted and direct 'on the job' training for a protégée.

Solutions

1 You must know your own goals and objectives before deciding what to delegate.
2 Select the jobs and match them to the personnel available.
3 Communicate with clarity the result (not the method) you require.

4   Ask for progress reports.
5   Beware of upward delegation in yourself and others — for if you take problems to the Boss instead of answers — then your colleagues will probably do the same to you.

You may find, especially in a small school, that there is indeed no-one to delegate to. Then perhaps you should not have accepted the job in the first place.

The inability to say NO

We continually accept assignments beyond our ability to complete in the limited time we have. Can they be done by others or even not at all? Why do we do this?
- We want to help others and gain approval.
- We have a fear of offending others.

How to say no!

1   **Listen** — you may be asked to do something you really want to do!
2   **Say no** — not maybe or I'll come back to you.
3   If appropriate give **Reasons**
4   If possible offer **Alternatives**

PUT THEM ON A CARD on your desk.

- We think that saying yes will give us a good-guy image, win friends, influence people, make others indebted to us, enhance our prospects for promotion.
- Not having our own priorities clear: there's no reason to say no, not even an excuse.

Consequence
- We spend all day getting things done for others rather than achieving our own objectives.
- Remember your best excuse is prior commitment to your own and your school's priorities.
- Recognise that if we fail to get our work done we may lose rather than gain respect.

People who are effective at their work do not offend others by saying NO when it is necessary.

Suggestion

Activity 4
Identify one definable task that you currently wish to achieve in your role as coordinator. If possible, break it down into a sub-set of smaller tasks. Estimate how long the achievement of the whole task and the subtasks will take. Identify when you will probably have time to complete the tasks. Construct a clear agenda within your available total time for the achievement of the things you need to do. Do it!

Procrastination

Everyone is an expert at putting things off. Causes are likely to be forgetfulness and a preference for doing pleasant tasks first. This leads to a habit of leaving difficult tasks until later. Perpetrators exhibit a lack of self discipline, a failure to set deadlines, easily fall prey to distractions, and leave tasks unfinished. Delay seems excusable and mistakes intolerable so procrastination can be the result of the fear of making errors. Perfection is unattainable however, and mistakes detected early or at least on-time are far more easily dealt with than those discovered at the last minute.

Solutions

- Set deadlines and go public by announcing them.
- Schedule the difficult, the important, the unpleasant jobs first.

Personal qualities

There are those who argue that

 individual and organisational development are not separate and discrete, but co-exist in a mutually supportive relationship.

(*Professional Development for Educational Management*, Kydd, Crawford and Riches, 1997)

Key personal skills which coordinators will need to develop in order to promote their subject, can be listed as:

- an ability to empathise with those threatened;

   Campbell (1985) has described difficulties in the coordinators' role particularly arising from their limited influence in altering their colleagues' classroom practices. Forms of hostility are detected, some of which are linked to a perception by classteachers of a reduction in their own autonomy.

- to act consistently;

   No-one is prepared to follow a leader who chops and changes with the wind and who is so unpredictable that it

---

The skills necessary to be a 'good mother', 'good wife', and 'good woman', are many of the same skills necessary to be a good manager and leader — for both male and female teachers.

Hall (1996) *Dancing on the Ceiling*

---

seems they are never content. Consistency in coordinating your subject might be shown by a willingness to look with teachers at their termly plans; a steady and calm approach to inevitable misunderstandings; timely pursuit of one goal at a time; and praise when teachers succeed in areas they had previously found difficult.

■ to maintain hope, belief and optimism;

The **can do** approach attracts success with which others will wish to be associated. Those who see the way ahead full of opportunities rather than problems; who see partial success as a result rather than a failure, will win converts. No one likes a moaning, pessimistic malcontent. Believe in your colleagues, look forward to achievements, pursue a positive vision.

■ to want success;

If the target foremost in your mind is children's improvement in using IT in your subject, or in a wider use of AT1 in science to investigate physical phenomena, your actions will naturally be geared towards its achievement. If, however, you are not particularly bothered whether or not data bases are used in science, or whether or not Year 2 ever do go outside for games — it will show.

■ to be willing to take calculated risks and accept the consequences;

Taking risks means being bold in inviting in speakers; making a decision about soft or hardware rather than sitting on the fence; making a strong recommendation to your colleagues; and setting courageous targets for yourself and others. Gain without pain is rare indeed and taking a safe path will mean that your achievements although positive may be moderate. Coordinators need to be fairly thick skinned 'when colleagues performed well the post holder received little credit; when they went badly he or she took the blame' (Campbell, 1985, p. 68–76). We do not achieve success by insuring against failure.

■ to develop a capacity to accept, deal with and use conflict constructively;

If everything was a smooth route to inevitable improvement, then the computers would currently be seen everywhere being used effectively, all the children would know their tables and teachers' walls would be covered in high quality geography field work. Your position would not be necessary. If the situation is less than perfect it is quite possible that some people have avoided facing up to children's current needs and will continue to do so unless challenged. Who is there to force the issue except you? Conflict may arise. Can you use this effectively?

■ to learn to use a soft voice and low key manner;

This is the antidote to the above. Of course, it is true that persuasion is better than coercion. You will need to cultivate a tolerance of ambiguity and complexity and when dealing with colleagues, recognising that issues are seldom black or white. In a world of constant change a high tolerance of ambiguity and acceptance of temporariness are required (Whitaker 1997). Striking a balance consists of centring on some aspects and being content with partial success in others. The difficult part, of course, is knowing which is which!

■ to develop self-awareness;

Can you find out what others make of your efforts to date? You need to grow to appreciate your own strengths and weaknesses. The willingness of your colleagues to accept advice also depends on their perception of your ability in the classroom. Teachers will also make judgments as to the value of the advice based on the coordinator's range of experience, ability to organise resources, knowledge of the subject and range of interpersonal skills.

■ to make strategic compromises;

Accommodating your expectations to the reality of just what can be achieved is a sign of maturity. An effective compromise, being content to allow some teachers to use just a narrow range of software or a employ limited range of communications technology until they feel sufficiently competent to move on, might be just such a compromise.

- to become an active listener.

    Listen to people and discover what motivates others. If you talk all the time you will never find out. We want to encourage children to develop listening skills, so we should not ignore our own advice. Seeing a problem from another's standpoint may make the solution apparent.

- to learn to match advice to individual teacher's needs not necessarily your own preferred approach.

    Galton (1995) argues that for in-service training to be effective in changing practice we must approach individual teachers differentially and offer them just enough to help them to the next stage, not overwhelm them with either the best possible practice or the particular approach of the coordinator. Teachers new to the class management issues raised by the continuous use of ICT or aspects of PE for example, may not be able to grasp the reasons behind your expert approach to a problem and will put down your success to characteristics such as personality and conclude that the approach is beyond them. Competent and more experienced teachers however, may well benefit from involvement with you in their classrooms in the same way that competent musicians improve through attendance at master classes.

This atmosphere can be maintained only where changes introduced are consistently seen to benefit children throughout the school rather than merely to advantage the reputation of the initiator. A professional approach to leading colleagues is well described in an article by Marion Dadds (1997) in 'School improvement inside out'.

Effective communication

Some coordinators may find that their opportunities to influence colleagues are limited. You may soon discover that the method you use to get your message across may be as important as the content itself. It may help to establish some principles for effective communication. The following list is based on Joan Dean's (1987) book *Managing the Primary School*.

- Teachers are more likely to be responsive to the advice of coordinators if addressed personally rather than anonymously in a staff meeting or by memo.
- Coordinators will need to learn that with teachers, just as with children, rousing the interest of the listener is necessary in order to get your message across.
- Information is more likely to be valued if it gives some clear advantages to the listener.
- No-one likes to be seen as letting down their team or working group. It is desirable therefore sometimes for coordinators to present their information in such a way that it requires action upon which others will rely.
- Teachers charged with the responsibility of promoting curricular areas to their colleagues may find an advantage in choosing an appropriate messenger. The status of the source of the information is often seen to indicate its importance.
- The situation (surroundings, time of day etc.) should be chosen carefully in order to predispose the listener to be receptive.

Making meetings effective

Meetings are the most common method that coordinators use in an attempt to get their message over, but they are not always a success. Just having a meeting is not enough. The prime consideration must be: *What do you want to happen at the meeting?* This point is seldom addressed, for many meetings need never happen at all.

You may need to call a meeting:

- to communicate information
  Subject coordinators will often need to give information to their colleagues, such as the dates and location of a local history and geography book exhibition, the list of computer programs bought by the PTA, and so on. Often this information can be given out in written form with only a brief explanation needed, possibly without having

a meeting at all. The skill you will need to develop is to ensure that the information is read and acted upon. Wasting everyone's time for an hour, to compensate for your lack of foresight in not preparing a briefing sheet however, does not go down well with busy teachers.

- **to generate discussion**

  If you want teachers to discuss issues, they need to have been properly prepared beforehand by being given the relevant information. You may need to arrange the seating in such a way that everyone can see each other in order to encourage participation. A brainstorming session recorded on tape can generate ideas or possible solutions.

  The key to success for this type of meeting is to create an atmosphere which encourages staff to share ideas and perceptions. They will not do this if early statements (even when inappropriate) are not accepted, at least as starting points for the generation of further ideas.

- **to make corporate decisions**

  If coordinators are organising a meeting to reach a decision on a key topic it is vital that everyone is made aware that the meeting has this purpose. Time has to be allowed beforehand, such that small group meetings can already have aired some of the issues. Make sure teachers have had time to read and absorb printed material. Decide before the meeting if you intend to take a vote if necessary, or whether it would be more appropriate to continue the debate until a consensus is reached.

To run a successful meeting:
- clarify objectives;
- emphasise the equality of each participant;
- be prepared to put forward your own opinions. Be honest yourself and expect others to be so;
- encourage contributions by both verbal and non-verbal behaviour such as eye contact;
- encourage members to listen to each other by listening yourself;
- praise other people for their contributions;
- regularly review what has been said;
- ask open-ended questions;
- sum up and conclude and check with the team that you are reflecting their views;
- ensure that recommendations are written up on large sheets of paper;
- thank team members; and,
- congratulate yourself on a job well done!

Dunham (1995)

Coordinators will hold more effective meetings if they understand the difference between the various purposes of these staff meetings and realise what can go wrong. We have all attended meetings which were monopolised by one person, had too many important items left to the end, or failed to get people involved. Occasionally all these things happen in the one meeting. We have also all attended well-run friendly and relaxed meetings which kept to the point and seemed like time well spent.

Coordinators need to consider a variety of strategies for organising and chairing meetings. Their aim should be to ensure that as many as possible of the negative features are avoided and the positive ones achieved. In *The Primary School Management Book* (Playfoot, Skelton and Southworth, 1989) further useful information can be found on the conduct of effective meetings in school.

INSET for yourself and your colleagues

The development of your team is, of course, central to the improvement of teaching. Indeed according to exponents of Total Quality Management Systems, widely acclaimed in industry for more productive working,

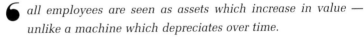 *all employees are seen as assets which increase in value — unlike a machine which depreciates over time.*

(Greenwood and Gaunt, 1994)

For the professional development of colleagues in your subject or area you will certainly need to keep yourself aware, and take advantage of all of the INSET opportunities available. If you are to be able to act as a resource for your staff you will need to develop contacts and sources of help. Personal contacts and sources of information are built up slowly through attending courses and building relationships with those in equivalent positions to yourself. For newcomers a local network of coordinators may exist already and may be of help in sorting out local problems and finding out about good quality INSET. But it is possible that you will have to plan, facilitate and deliver training sessions, yourself.

In order to gain the support of colleagues many coordinators have:
- organised INSET days;
- arranged regular times to be available for consultation;
- supported teachers' own applications to attend INSET;
- put on demonstrations of materials and children's work at lunchtimes;
- advised at team/year group curriculum planning meetings;
- checked and commented on teachers' termly work forecasts;
- worked alongside teachers in their classrooms;
- arranged visits to other schools to see their subject in action;
- arranged for the loan of materials for teachers to use at home;
- put up displays of children's work; and, arranged software loans for trials.

Alan and Sue Cross (1993) give a step by step template for a successful INSET day in any subject — and the key to their approach is in the planning and preparation for the time available to be used to maximum effect. INSET events take various forms, but when we are considering whole-school development, of the sort discussed in this handbook, a day spent with colleagues examining your own situation with your own problems, with your own children in mind, can be invaluable. However, six hours of your colleagues' time is expensive and this knowledge can make organising such an event intimidating even for the most experienced member of staff. The following points whilst not ensuring success, will mean that progress is more likely.

Aims for the session

Consider the outcome for the day. What will your colleagues know, be able to do, understand that they did not know before? Will their attitudes have changed, will new ways of working have become established? Discuss the position with other significant people on the staff and try to establish an aim. Write this down in a sentence or two and look through your file to see how well this fits with your monitoring conclusions, the School Development Plan (SDP) etc. Is the session to develop or use a new resource; to create or implement a curriculum document; to establish an organisational system to plan a parents' meeting? The imminent arrival of an OFSTED team may sharpen the concentration of your team. How will you use this to your advantage? Let everyone know that this is its purpose. You will be more likely to achieve the aim if everyone shares it with you.

Prepare and circulate a simple proposal for the day.
You might include:

- an anecdote or an ice breaking activity;
- an introduction (which may include a statement of aims and rationale for those aims);
- some targeted practical activities, perhaps not all introduced by you;
- some brainstorming and the use of these suggestions;
- group work where agreed decisions are reached;
- snowballing (where pairs, then fours, then larger groups discuss key points);
- plenary sessions which develop key ideas at the end of each main block of time;
- recaps and reminders as you move into new areas and after breaks;
- appropriate flexibility (of both time and content);
- visits to parts of the school (such as a resource base) or further afield;
- time to consider management of the initiative in the classroom (this is often a key issue);
- well-prepared resources (you may need to borrow items, beware of relying on other people);
- an outsider (advisory teacher, teacher, adviser, college or university lecturer);
- the phasing of practical and talking sessions;
- collaboration with another school (think of advantages and disadvantages);
- needs of teachers of early years and those who work with older children;
- a conclusion which makes participants feel their time has been well spent.

It is often a good idea to include coffee breaks within periods for practical work. Remember that teachers do need a break! It is better to work hard for a shorter period than prolong the activities.

Make sure that:

- everyone knows the arrangements, including part-time and temporary and secretarial staff;
- non-teaching staff are aware of what is happening and why;
- any printing is done in advance of the day, with extra copies of everything;
- that the proposed room will be large enough, the right temperature and comfortable (small chairs can cause considerable discomfort);
- any documents required will be available;
- stationery is on hand;
- videos and computers work — check them the previous day and again immediately before you start; and,
- lunch arrangements are made and agreed.

Set the tone:

- show that you are interested in how colleagues feel;
- if you are younger or new to the school, be aware that you may appear to be a great threat to colleagues who have taught for many years, so be seen to take advice;
- prepare everything prior to the day. You may be able to negotiate some time for this, but don't expect it;
- where possible and relevant do related work with your children prior to the event; don't ask people to do what you have not done or are not prepared to do in the classroom; and,
- it may be worth circulating an article, notes or a prompt sheet prior to the event.

Professional development days can create an enormous momentum in the school. These events always need following up. They are never an end in themselves. Time is a precious commodity so it is essential that the day is viewed as a success and that there is a positive outcome with realistic, achievable targets.

Gaining and managing a budget

You will need to ask to control and account for a small budget to support your promotion of teaching and learning in your subject. You will then be able to buy and use resources without continual recourse to your head. Arrange to find a method of gaining agreement amongst the staff for the use of this money. Record the results of any meetings (formal and informal) you have had to determine spending of this fund and include this record with an end-of-year account of what the money was spent on and give this in to the head even if she doesn't ask for it. Can you make a judgment as to the value for the money spent in last year's budget? Were the books of more use than the CD-ROM drive? Which apparatus was the most welcomed? Should you have bought two flat maps rather than one globe? Make sure that you show that you have considered such issues when you write up your report on last year's spending.

Producing arguments for resourcing your subject will need to be one of your higher priority endeavours especially if, like say ICT or the library, it can be a very expensive area of activity. In producing a budget or bid for funding you will need to take account of particular local circumstances, such as the disposition of the senior management team to pupil's achievements in your subject and the current extent of the use of equipment, books and facilities you already have in the school. Below are some issues you might find useful to pursue.

■ What is the ratio of children to computers, books, games equipment in your school? How does this compare nationally? This information may be available through the information sent to schools when being inspected or may be published by your subject association or local group. How much time per day does this allow in your subject? How many children can use other resources simultaneously? Is the level of resources driving the teaching methodology? What would OFSTED say about this? Can you formulate an argument for greater resourcing? Is infrequent use of science or DT apparatus leading to superficial and fragmented use? Is damage being done to sensitive equipment by wheeling it about every day? Are there inefficiencies in timetabling of resources such as the library or PE space or is the housing of resources causing a problem? Does the school have the most modern machines, post-Dearing text books, sufficient reading materials for implementation of the literacy and numeracy hours? (*'Do we at Falmer Primary always have to appear to be so far behind St Johns?'* is a line some coordinators might find useful). Is there a particular group of children in the school who would especially benefit from exclusive use of some materials, which would justify a better than normal ratio?

■ Would the purchase of ROAMERS or PIP replace the use of floor turtles and thereby release computers for other purposes? Are areas of the curriculum dealing with angles and degrees of turn being sufficiently well taught?

■ Do the prospectuses of neighbouring schools proudly detail the sports facilities? Parents are often impressed by such details. Could the school brochure or newsletter be better produced with the help of new equipment, could expenditure on better quality art paper and materials have a beneficial effect on the school's environment? If you can persuade your head that there is an advantage to be gained in such matters your path may be smoother.

■ Use National Curriculum requirements to enhance your arguments. If children need to be able to find and present information, then they will need to have the means to do so. And this not just once but as part of their everyday experience.

Your budget request should be quite clear about what benefits can be expected from various levels of funding. It should be divided into three sections.

1 **Rationale**
   This section should briefly describe the contribution your subject currently makes to the quality of children's learning in your school, its potential for the future and the money spent on it in previous years.

2 **Repair, maintenance and consumables**
   Once you have worked out a budget for repairs and maintenance after day to day wear and tear on equipment you need to consider requesting other sums under this heading. Maintenance means having the ability to continue being able to do the things next year that you did in this. Thus you need to take account of depreciation and

replacement costs, and put money aside each financial year to pay for the eventual replacement of the equipment, books and apparatus you have already.

If your subject has many cross-curricular links and the order of topics has changed, you will still want to be able to offer the same degrees of support in a variety of curriculum areas and topic work that you have done in the past. Ask for money rather than specific materials, as the detail will not become apparent until after teachers have held their planning meetings at various times during the year. Finally, remember the cost of consumables as you will need to work out just how much in the way of materials will be necessary for teaching the subjects.

3   Development

This is the part of the budget bid in which you demonstrate the benefits which would accrue to the children if additional money was spent on your subject. The most appropriate of the arguments presented at the start of this section come to the fore here along with any needs thrown up in discussion with classteachers.

It can be effective to quote other teachers when presenting these issues:

- *'The lower juniors consider that. . . .'*
- *'The equipment in the nursery is particularly prone to breakdown and Mrs Bright feels . . .'*
- *'The Yr 6 team were telling me. . . .'*

or use ghosts

- *'The government expects us to . . .'*
- *'Parents have often commented that . . . :'*
- *'OFSTED always make a point of commenting on . . .'*

or use National Curriculum pressures to your advantage:

- *'xxx skills appear in the National Curriculum documents for . . . subjects'*
- *'The SAT results for our school show that more work will be needed in . . .'*

If you intend to make a case for the purchase of one or more additional pieces of equipment have all the details to hand so that no-one can shelve your request, claiming the need to wait for further information. Get local dealers to send you details of lease-purchase agreements which would avoid having to meet the costs of buying capital equipment from one single year's budget.

A budget plan

1   Take the priorities from the school development plan and match them to your spending requirements.
2   Ask teachers to list their own needs and then prioritise them.
3   Place orders with most appropriate supplier and keep a record.
4   Monitor the effect of your spending and evaluate the financial decisions you have taken.

The tables on pages 55–58 are examples of forms which can be used to track and monitor your budget management.

Suggestion

Activity 5
Consider the skills you need to develop to be a more effective coordinator. Ideally, you should have abilities in the following skills and attributes. Audit your current state of development by rating yourself on the chart below. Add these ratings to your coordinator's file.

Positive comments   **Aspects in need of development**

Ability to prioritise
Ability to delegate
Leading/chairing meetings
Organisational skills
Managing your time
Listening to others
Tact and diplomacy
Assertiveness
Communication skills
Study and research skills
Enthusiasm, drive, determination
Negotiation/discussion skills
Assertiveness
Being positive and encouraging others
Sense of humour, stress management
Receptiveness to new and other's ideas

Subject:	Academic year:		Compiled by:	
Cost estimate SDP Priority targets	maintenance	replacement	consumables	development
1				
2				
3				
4				
Totals				

© Falmer Press

FIG 3.1
Budget planning: school priorities

Subject: Academic year: Compiled by:

Cost estimate teacher's own requirements	maintenance items	replacements needed	consumables please list	development agreed	revised costs	priority
1						
2						
3						
4						
5						
6						

© Falmer Press

FIG 3.2
Budget Planning: teacher's requests

keeping track of your orders

Items ordered	Cost	Order number	Supplier and date	Delivery signed by: date	Delivery note no	Invoice amount	Invoice no date	Running totals	Destination of items
1									
2									
3									
4									
5									
6									

© Falmer Press

FIG 3.3
Budget planning: order inventory

Spending in year:		Subject:		Complied by:	
GEST spending items			Purchases		
Course: attended by:		Effect/result	Item purchased: Cost:		*Effect/result*

© Falmer Press

FIG 3.4
Budget planning: monitoring spending effectiveness

Part two

How the inspection process works

| Chapter 4 | Your role before and after the inspection |

> ❝ Public accountability is important ... however ... successful schools are those which reflect upon their own practice and devise and implement changes in response to the needs of their pupils. Some of the most valuable strategies for improvement are those initiated by the school community itself.
>
> The National Commission on Education (1993) p. 170

It is useful to consider the OFSTED inspection process in three stages:

- what happens before the actual week in which the inspection team are in your school;
- what happens during the inspection week; and,
- what happens as a result of the inspection when the inspectors have left the school.

In this part, each of the stages of the inspection process will be described and the ways in which there is an impact on, or involvement of, subject coordinators will be highlighted. This will enable you to check back to the analysis of your role completed as one of the activities in the previous chapters and track forward to the next parts, which are concerned with the detailed ways in which you can improve and enhance your performance as a coordinator.

The inspection team

For the purposes of this book it is not necessary to go into great detail about the ways in which a school inspection is set up. Suffice to say that the contractor, be it an LEA, university, consortium or private firm who has won the contract to inspect your school will engage a registered inspector and inspection team to carry out the inspection. It is quite possible that none of the team, who may be three or more people, including a 'lay' inspector, will have met before they arrive on the premises and will all have varied experience of the job they are about to do. The Registered Inspector will contact the headteacher to agree a week during which direct observation will take place. Various other meetings will be arranged — with staff, parents and the governing body and a date will be set for the collection of pre-inspection documentation.

The OFSTED inspection schedule
1   Main findings
2   Key issues for action
3   Introduction:
       3.1 Characteristics of the school
       3.2 Key Indicators

Aspects of the school
4   Educational standards achieved by pupils at the school
       4.1 Attainment and progress
       4.2 Attitudes, behaviour and personal development
       4.3 Attendance
5   Quality of education provided
       5.1 Teaching
       5.2 The curriculum and assessment
       5.3 Pupils' spiritual, moral, social and cultural development
       5.4 Support, guidance and pupils' welfare
       5.5 Partnership with parents and the community
6   The management and efficiency of the school
       6.1 Leadership and management
       6.2 Staffing, accommodation and resources
       6.3 The efficiency of the school

Curriculum areas and subjects
7   Areas of learning for children under five
8   English, mathematics and science
9   Other subjects

Inspection data
10 Summary of inspection evidence
11 Data and indicators

The pre-inspection meeting between staff and Registered Inspector is an opportunity to clarify the detail and protocol of the inspection week. For example, you will wish to know something of the timing, nature and extent of the coordinator's interview. And it is reassuring to know that if inspectors aren't smiling when they enter your room its probably because they don't want to be there any more than you do. How many inspectors will be involved and for how long depends on the number of pupils in the school, with slight adjustments for any special circumstances, such as there being a special unit of some kind in your school. For an average sized primary school it is likely that you will have four or five inspectors in school for about four days. One of the inspectors will be the lay inspector, a person who has had no previous professional contact with schools. (However, Hustler and Stone (1996) have found that most lay persons so trained have been unsuccessful in finding work and those who have are constantly used in inspection teams and, because of this, are likely to have become 'cultural insiders' at the very least). Lay inspectors tend to spend less time in school and frequently do not inspect the curriculum. However, as with all elements of the inspection process, there will be variations in the way teams operate and it is made quite clear in the legislation that lay inspectors are able to inspect any part of the framework.

Before the inspection the Registered Inspector, who is the leader of the inspection team, will deploy his or her team in respect of what has to be inspected under the inspection schedule. The schedule is set out here in the order in which the inspection report on the school must be written.

Typical OFSTED Inspection Team Deployment

RgI (4 days)
    Science, Design and Technology, IT, PE, SEN
    Main findings, Key issues

3.1 Characteristics
3.2 Key Indicators
5.1 Quality of teaching
6.3 Efficiency
6.2 Staffing accommodation and learning resources
Lay Inspector (2 days)
4.3 Attendance
5.3 Spiritual, social and moral development
5.4 Support guidance and pupils' welfare
5.5 Partnership with parents and the community
Team inspector (4 days)
English, history, geography, art
5.2 Curriculum and assessment
4.2 Attitudes behaviour and personal development
Team Inspector/deputy RgI (4 days)
U5s, mathematics, music, RE, equality of opportunity
4.1 Attainment and progress
6.1 Management and leadership

The additional requirements concerned with school improvement and progress made since a previous inspection, introduced from September 1998 for primary schools, have been referred to in Chapter 1. There are also revised procedures for inspecting and reporting on teaching, which include a requirement for Registered Inspectors to offer feedback to teachers about their teaching which was observed. All teachers receive a confidential summary of their teaching grades under three categories — excellent or very good, good or satisfactory, less than satisfactory. These are given in respect of each lesson and therefore judgments about the quality of their teaching in each subject is known to the individual teacher. The headteacher receives, also in confidence, a summary of this information. This summary is regarded by OFSTED as an important management tool.

We have already indicate that the evidence on which judgments about the performance of the school in part A of the Framework, aspects of the school, will be based, and that it will come in large part from what is discovered about part B, the curriculum areas and subjects. We know that the key elements of the schedule affecting the subject coordinator's role, as well as their own subjects, are concentrated in those aspects concerned with curriculum and assessment and leadership and

Detailed elaboration of the schedule is contained in the OFSTED handbook: *Guidance on the Inspection of Nursery and Primary Schools* (OFSTED, 1995) and you should refer to it for further information.

Inspection Report

Throughout the school literacy and numeracy across the curriculum is under used and unsatisfactory. However, pupils with special educational needs make satisfactory progress in relation to their prior attainment.

Extract from an OFSTED report:
One form entry primary school —
November 1997

management. However, there will be a relationship between all parts of the schedule and your subject(s), which will be highlighted in more detail in the next chapter.

From September 1997, it has been a requirement of inspection contracts that each individual inspector taking the lead in inspecting or coordinating the evidence and judgments in particular subjects and aspects, must be identified in the published inspection report. Thus it will be clear to teachers and other readers which inspector played the key role in writing each section of the report. However, overall responsibility for the published report remains with the Registered Inspector.

All inspectors will be required to consider equal opportunities issues and the provision made for pupils with special educational needs. Also, the key skills of oracy, literacy, numeracy and information technology will be reported upon specifically and all inspectors will be keen to evaluate how well these skills are taught throughout the curriculum and in all subjects.

Despite the separation of reporting responsibilities, the judgments the inspection team make are required to be corporate and team members will be continually sharing their evidence and judgments before and during the inspection week. The Registered Inspector is responsible for making sure that the inspection adheres to the requirements of the inspection framework and is conducted in a proper manner. He or she must ensure that all members of the inspection team abide by the Code of Conduct which governs the inspection process and which is set out in the inspection handbook.

The Code of Conduct stipulates that inspectors should:
- carry out their work with professionalism, integrity and courtesy;
- evaluate the work of the school objectively;
- report honestly and fairly;
- communicate clearly and frankly;
- act in the best interests of the pupils of the school;
- respect the confidentiality of personal information received during the inspection.

(OFSTED 1994a)

Before the inspection

When the dates on which the inspection team will be in school have been agreed, the Registered Inspector will set up an initial visit to the school. He or she will meet with the headteacher and staff and the governing body of the school to discuss the inspection process, to answer any queries and to invite the headteacher and governing body to identify any particular issues they would like the governing body to focus on, provided that it can be done within the scope of the framework and the particular contract for the school.

There will also be a meeting for parents of pupils at the school without the headteacher, staff and governors being present — unless of course they are also parents with children in the school. At the meeting the Registered Inspector will invite parents to express their views about the school according to a set agenda, which is included in the inspection guidance handbook. The RgI will explain to parents the reasons for the meeting and answer questions; seek parents' views about the school; and note (but not comment on the validity of) those views. In particular, inspectors will ask parents to comment on:

- pupils' attainment and the progress they make;
- the attitudes and values promoted by the school;
- the information which the school provides, including reports on pupils' progress;
- the help and guidance given to pupils;
- homework and the contribution it makes to pupils' progress;
- the behaviour and attendance of pupils;
- the part parents play in the life of the school; and,
- the school's response to their suggestions and complaints.

The school is also invited to issue a questionnaire for parents which further seeks information as to their feelings about the school. A summary of the responses to the questionnaire will be included in the inspection report. The views which parents hold about the school are regarded as potentially important

---

Inspection Report

Provision for pupils' spiritual, moral and cultural development is sound. Pupils have opportunities and time to reflect upon the work they are doing. However, the school does not yet fully implement their stated policy. Pupils know what to do if subject to persistent bullying and the school is responsive to any incidents. Parents expressed concern about this matter and the school will need to build parents' confidence that such matters are dealt with effectively. Pupils have the opportunity to take responsibility, for example by running a school bank, and take care of one another, when hurt or upset. Social development is encouraged by a number of clubs and after school activities including representing the school in sports teams.

Primary school — November 1997

Suggestion

Activity 6
What steps has your school taken, with particular reference to your own area of responsibility, to make parents aware of your aims and provision? Consider information in your school's prospectus; any documentation for parents specifically about your area; and curriculum workshops held.

evidence which inspectors can use in supporting their judgments. Since September 1997, it has been a requirement of the inspection process that the Registered Inspector must refer to any significant positive views or concerns expressed by parents and any inspection findings relating to them. They must be reported back to the school's senior management team and to its governing body, as well as being included in the final inspection report.

The Registered Inspector will at this stage wish to receive any documentation which it has been agreed that the school will make available before the inspection in school. This documentation is used to give the inspection team a background to the inspection and to help the Registered Inspector to identify any particular issues on which the inspection might need to focus. The documentation which is likely to be required is listed in the OFSTED guidance handbook.

The following documents will be requested:
- a completed headteacher's form and statement;
- school prospectus;
- school development plan or other planning document;
- copy of last governors' annual report to parents;
- minutes of governing body (or other) for the last 12 months;
- staff handbook (if available);
- curriculum plans, policies and guidelines or schemes of work, already in existence;
- other policy documents available in the school;
- a programme or timetable of the work of the school for the period of the inspection;
- other information the school wishes to be considered, including self evaluations.

Documents which are likely to have most relevance for your role in school will be curriculum plans, policies and guidelines and schemes of work. These will include subject documents but also general policies such as those on teaching and learning; assessment; equal opportunities; special educational needs; multi-cultural education, all of which clearly have a bearing on subject provision.

Parents' questionnaires						
		strongly agree	agree	neither	disagree	strongly disagree
1	I feel that the school encourages parents to play an active part in the life of the school					
2	I would find it easy to approach the school with problems or questions to do with my child(ren)					
3	The school handles complaints from parents well					
4	The school gives me a clear understanding of what is taught					
5	The school keeps me well informed about my child(ren)'s progress					
6	The school enables my children to achieve a good standard of work					
7	The school encourages children to get involved in more than just their daily lessons					
8	I am satisfied with the work my child(ren) is/are expected to do at home					
9	The school's values have a positive effect on my child(ren)					
10	The school achieves a high standard of good behaviour					
11	My child(ren) like(s) school					

reproduced with permission of OFSTED

Suggestion

Activity 7

Make a provisional audit of any documentation you know of in your school which you think may have relevance to your coordinator responsibilities. Check out your list with colleagues to ensure the comprehensiveness and consistency of your knowledge.

Of course, inspectors' judgments about the usefulness of your documentation will depend upon how good they think it is: essentially, to the extent to which they feel it contributes to the quality of education provided in your subject area. It is seldom judged in its own right. Thus schools preparing for an inspection are far wiser to spend any extra effort in fully implementing the policies and plans they already have rather than inventing new ones which, by their failure to impact upon practice, will probably attract criticism. Part 3 of this book gives detailed guidance on policy, policy formation and documentation.

The Headteacher's Form, completed to a standard format prior to the inspection and an important part of the pre-inspection evidence, contains basic data on the school which includes National Curriculum assessment results. This is very important data which has to be included prominently in the inspection report. It will certainly form a starting point for inspectors

Activity 8

If assessment and test results data is available for a subject for which you have coordinator responsibility, gather it together as a basis for analysis.

Consider — why are the results the way they are? Is there a plan of action to improve these results?

Activity 9

Obtain a copy of your school's current school development plan and plans for any previous years. Identify any references to your subject area in the plans. Any targets or success criteria in them for your subject can form the basis for analysis of where you are up to as you come to make specific position statements and/or action plans.

The sound performance of individual teachers does not lead to the rate of pupil progress necessary because the work is too uncoordinated and the curriculum lacking in certain aspects. No systems are in place to ensure that pupils receive their curriculum entitlement. The teachers do not work as a team delivering a coherent programme and National Curriculum requirements are not fully met in English, IT, history, and geography. In D&T requirements are barely met. Lack of effective across key stage planning means that there are differences in the way these and other subjects are implemented for children in different classes. The lack of appropriate guidance, and the absence of secure links to the National Curriculum mean that in many of these subjects coverage is not sufficient. Thus the overall effect of individual teachers' efforts is unsatisfactory.

One form entry primary school, October 1998

---

in the core subjects of English, mathematics and science. Many schools also carry out standardised testing procedures, particularly in reading and English and mathematics. Where data generated by such testing is available, it will be of interest to inspectors.

The analysis of assessment results should form an important part, among other things, of your procedures for monitoring how your school is performing in your subject. You may use the PANDAs (Performance and Assessment Data) and OFSTED's (1998) *School Evaluation Matters* to help you. Monitoring and evaluation structures in general and the analysis of assessment data are dealt with at greater length in Part 4 and other books in the series give subject specific advice.

The Registered Inspector will also require a copy of your school's development plan (SDP). This may or may not include references to your subject or area of responsibility. If it does, you should be aware of it, hopefully because you were responsible for it, although if you are new to a school or new to the particular subject coordinator role, this may not be the case. The action plan for your subject might usefully be reviewed if your subject is a priority in the SDP. You should always be clear about the state of development with regard to your subject or area of responsibility, and you will wish to be doubly sure about this at the time of your school's inspection, which represents an unprecedentedly rigorous external audit of its performance. Action planning and how it relates to your coordinating role is dealt with in detail in Part 4.

The Registered Inspector will also require information on the school's budget, which is integral to the development plan. Again, your subject may in some way be part of the budget plan and your potential role in identifying and meeting resource needs is dealt with in Chapter 7.

As you can see, the inspection team is armed with a great deal of information before it carries out the direct inspection in school. As a coordinator you will have made an important contribution to the quality of that information. The time to prepare this is well in advance of the request for documents.

Before the inspection the Registered Inspector will ask for school and class timetables of teaching programmes for the inspection period to be made available. It is important for coordinators to check these and to ascertain exactly what is going to take place in their subjects in order that a valid picture of the work that normally goes on is presented. Coordinators should check that the work is related to, and drawn down from, long- and medium-term plans. The short-term plans for the inspection week will vary according to the subject. Inspectors will make it clear that they will expect to see teaching of the core National Curriculum subjects and whatever else the school does as part of its normal programme for the period of the inspection. There is no requirement for the school to adjust its curriculum, but what that curriculum is should be carefully planned. For example, a coordinator for information technology may wish to discuss with colleagues exactly what IT they will be using to support the subjects at the time of the inspection and to be aware of the balance presented between the different IT strands. Where there are gaps, evidence for their presence in the school should be available elsewhere, perhaps in planning, or pupils' work or in classroom and school displays of work. It may be useful for subject coordinators themselves to audit the IT in their subjects and liaise with the information technology coordinator. A similar overview process could be carried out by the relevant coordinators for other key skills of literacy and numeracy.

The Registered Inspector, before the inspection, should also give a clear indication of the kinds of discussions likely to be required with individual members of staff and the arrangements for looking at samples of pupils' work, current planning, pupils' records and reports, individual education plans for pupils with special educational needs and assessment documents. Guidance for coordinators on these matters is given in the next chapter, which looks at the inspection week itself.

After the inspection

In the next chapter we analyse in detail what happens in your school when the inspection team is undertaking direct

Suggestion

Activity 10
As a preparatory exercise, analyse the work you plan and carry out with your class for one week in order to identify where and to what extent your subject uses and develops the key skills of oracy, literacy, numeracy and information technology. Ask colleagues to do the same thing so that you gain initial information about how key skills are represented in your subject.

observation of the teaching and learning going on. At the end of the week you will breathe a sigh of relief as the team departs to finalise its judgments, write the draft report and identify the key issues for action which it considers the school will have to take. What the main findings and key issues are will depend upon the judgments of the inspection team and they are extremely variable. There is the possibility that a school will be found to be failing to provide, or that it is likely to fail to provide, a satisfactory quality of education for its pupils. Alternatively, where a school is providing a satisfactory education overall, it may be found to have serious weaknesses in some areas. In the case of a school failing its inspection or being found to have serious weaknesses specified procedures have to be followed, but in any case issues for action will be identified. We assume that matters are more straightforward, so that when this process is completed, and the time it takes varies between inspection teams, the Registered Inspector will give an oral report to the headteacher, and any other staff of the school whom the head wishes to invite, which will normally be your school's senior management team. The Registered Inspector will also meet your governing body to discuss the inspection findings. Both meetings take place before the written report on the school is finalised and the school has the opportunity to point out any factual errors which will be corrected in the report. At this stage there can be no negotiation about the judgments the inspection team have made.

In due course, and within a specified time scale, the full report will be published along with a summary of the main findings of the report, the key issues for action identified and an analysis of the parental questionnaire responses. This is the point at which the school is required to distribute the summary report to all parents and make clear the availability of the full report.

The governing body will then have eight working weeks to produce an action plan in response to the report, setting out the ways in which it intends to address the key issues. The extent to which you as a subject coordinator are involved in this will depend upon what the findings and issues for action are. If, for example, a key issue is to raise standards or enhance

Inspection Report

Some of the art taught is linked to other subjects which can limit the opportunity for teaching to focus on the key skills and elements of art. However, under the guidance of an enthusiastic art coordinator many single focus lessons are now undertaken and along with a soundly structured curriculum this allows pupils to consolidate and apply new skills and techniques that they learn. All the teaching seen in art lessons was good or very good. Some teaching emphasises the vocabulary of art and the knowledge and understanding of the skills and elements of art and this helps pupils to evaluate, modify and improve their work. Involvement of the coordinator in working alongside class teachers would make this more routine with a further positive effect on standards.

One form entry with nursery — September 1997

the quality of educational provision in an area of mathematics, and you are the coordinator for mathematics, you will certainly be heavily involved in the construction and implementation of the action plan. However, even if there is no significant reference to your subject in the Main Findings of the report and no Key Issues refer to it specifically, you will be keen to analyse the particular paragraph in the report which refers to your subject or area of responsibility. Often, Key Issues refer to general areas, for example assessment, which are relevant to all subjects areas, and you will need to consider the implications for your work.

All parents must receive a copy of the action plan, which will also go to OFSTED and your school's LEA. The governing body, in its annual report to parents, must comment upon progress towards achieving the targets of the action plan and in due course, when your school is re-inspected, the next group of inspectors will judge the extent to which the issues identified in the previous inspection have been dealt with. Indeed it will be the starting point for the next re-inspection of your school and include these judgments in the subsequent report. Action planning is dealt with in Part 3. The next chapter looks at the work of the inspection team whilst in your school.

Chapter 5 — The inspection team in your school

> ❝ *Charleston had the climate and ambience of Naples, but the wealth and style of a big American city . . . Every person was youthful, good-looking and well-scrubbed. It was like wandering into a Pepsi commercial . . . The promenade was crowded with cyclists and sweating joggers, who weaved expertly around the pedestrians and shuffling tourists . . . I walked back to my car, the sun warm on my back, and had the sneaking feeling that after such perfection things were bound to be downhill from now on.*
>
> Bill Bryson (1989) *The Lost Continent*

When the inspection team eventually arrives in your school they will be adding to the considerable amount of pre-inspection evidence they have already collected from the meetings and documentation described in the previous chapter. The principal way in which they will collect further information will be direct observation of teaching and pupils at work in their classrooms and other areas. This will take a majority of their time and will include talking with pupils about the work they are doing, as well as observing and assessing teaching. In practice, most inspection teams are likely to spend at least 60 per cent of their time in school in this kind of direct observation. As many as a hundred lessons or parts of lessons will be observed, varying according to the size of the school, which will take anything between 50 and 80 hours of inspection time. Regulations introduced in 1997 indicate that inspectors should carefully monitor the amount of time any individual teacher is observed. Around 50 per cent of lessons is regarded as an appropriate maximum.

Suggestion

Activity 11
What will be inspectors' first impression of your subject when they walk into your school? Are computers in evidence, does children's work in geography show in the displays, have teachers created a numerate environment, is literacy to the fore?
Walk about and imagine you are seeing the school for the first time. Ask parents, guests, students, teaching practice tutors, governors? What do they have to say about the priority given to your subject?

Inspectors will also hear a sample of at least 10 per cent of pupils read, recording their reading skills and strategies, their understanding and their ability to use their reading to find information and use libraries. They will scrutinise a representative sample of the recent work of pupils. They may well examine work in some specific areas, such as numeracy and information technology, through discussion with small groups of pupils. They will look at all of the teachers' plans, their records of National Curriculum tests and tasks and teacher assessments; the school's record-keeping systems; a sample of the annual written reports to parents; any baseline or entry tests or profiles which the school carries out; and, statements for pupils with special educational needs, their annual reviews and individual education plans.

Planned discussions will be held with the headteacher and deputy headteacher and members of staff with management responsibilities. This will include you in connection with your subject or area coordinating role.

The key elements on which the inspection will be focusing are:
- the standards being achieved by the pupils, especially their academic standards, and the progress in their learning that this represents;
- the quality and effectiveness of teaching in order to achieve high standards and good progress;
- the work and behaviour of the pupils in their response to the teaching; and,
- the effectiveness with which the school is led and managed.

As a coordinator you need to be aware of these key elements. Along with the other sections of the subject profile, these are the areas inspectors will be most likely to explore in their discussion\interview with you in your role as coordinator.

Discussions with coordinators

The first thing to be said about the coordinator interview is that there is no standard format for this and inspection teams will differ to some extent in the manner and organisation of the interviews and their focus. As suggested, the pre-inspection meeting with staff should provide a forum at which it will be possible for you to question inspectors about their approach and clarify what will be expected of you, so that you can be prepared for the particular style you will encounter. Some of the issues raised will be very specific and emanate from the detail of the inspection: clarification or exploration of something seen in the classroom, in pupils' work or in the pre-inspection documentation. However, you should be prepared to discuss and answer questions on all of the issues which follow.

1 **Your role and your perception of it**. How long you have been the subject coordinator; what is the content of your job description, if you have one, (try to avoid the classic response of a teacher to the opening question of one of the authors: '*What's a job description*?'); how you see your role; how committed you are to the tasks involved and how you go about them? You will, of course, be expected to talk about the detail of your subject or area of responsibility. You will not necessarily be expected to be an expert, but you will need to show a knowledge of the National Curriculum Programmes of Study and Attainment Targets and have a view about what constitutes quality in the teaching and learning of your subject. You will be expected to have a view on the standards currently being achieved in your subject, of the attainment and progress of pupils and the evidence upon which you base your views. You will want to be aware of the responses to and interest of pupils in your subject and perhaps give examples of ways in which it contributes to their behaviour, their attitudes and personal development and their spiritual, moral, social and cultural development, which will be easier or harder to identify in relation to the opportunities provided by the subject. For example, is there evidence of collaborative work, or respect for resources and the environment? Are there examples within your subject of pupils' cultural experience being widened, perhaps in history, music or art?

You should be aware of the strengths and weaknesses of the teaching of your subject throughout the school. Because teaching is seen as such a central issue and the quality of the teaching the inspectors find is a major factor in the whole inspection process and report, it is expanded upon in this chapter. Staff development and in-service training will have to be discussed. Who provides this and do you have a part to play in deciding which teacher should benefit from training in your subject?

You will need to be well briefed on the curriculum and assessment, especially how your subject forms part of the whole curriculum framework of the school. What policies, schemes and guidelines do you have? How much time is spent on your subject in each class and what assessment procedures are used? Are these consistent throughout the school? How is the issue of continuity and progression addressed? You will need to be clear about how your subject contributes to the key skills of oracy, literacy, numeracy and information technology. You will also need to be clear about how equal opportunity is ensured and how work in your subject is differentiated to meet the range of pupils' needs and abilities throughout the school and, in particular, how pupils' special educational needs are met.

You must be clear about resource provision in your subject or area. This will include the quality, quantity, range and appropriateness of resources and their general adequacy to meet curriculum requirement. You need to be aware of resource needs at the present time and how they are to be met. Is there sufficient staff expertise and are they qualified to support good quality provision and the achievement of high standards in your subject? Is the accommodation available suitable and appropriate for the teaching of your subject?

You should be aware of how your subject fits into the management of the whole school curriculum through its status in your school's development planning process. How do you fulfil the requirements of your role within this overall structure, how is your performance monitored (if it is) and importantly, how do you monitor and evaluate the work in your subject or area of responsibility?

Here we give two examples of the kind of questioning format an inspector might use during his or her interview with you in Figures 5.1a and 5.1b. The questions are by no means definitive but are intended to give you some indication of what you might expect.

Inspection Report

A good range of equipment to support scientific activity is documented, appropriately housed and accessible to teachers to implement the 2 year rolling programme. This plan however frequently commits every class to be studying very similar science topics during the same half term and puts pressure on science equipment when the whole school needs the same equipment and facilities at the same time. Part of the evaluation of the first year of the plan will need to examine this issue. The wild environmental area, inner garden and greenhouse enhance provision to teach the science curriculum.

Primary and nursery school — September 1997

Suggestion

Activity 12
Make preliminary answers to the questions posed and keep notes of them. You will already have thought about most of them when completing earlier activities. As you work through the handbook you will be able to extend and modify your answers.

FIG 5.1a
Coordinator interview questions

General role:
- How long have you been doing your job?
- Have you a job description, and if so how was it formulated?
- How could changes be made to the job description?
- How do other members of staff know what your role and responsibilities are?
- What situation did you inherit when you took over responsibility for your subject: were you starting from scratch or was it a going concern?

Standards and progress:
- What is your view of levels of achievement of pupils in your subject through the school?
- In which areas are standards and progress good?
- Are there areas where standards should be higher?
- How do your school's standards compare with national standards, local ones and with schools with similar characteristics to yours?
- Are there any significant trends in standards and progress over time?
- What provision is made for pupils with special educational needs and how do they perform?
- On what information do you base your knowledge of standards?

Curriculum and assessment:
- How were your policies and schemes of work developed?
- What are the mechanisms for policy review and further development?
- How is continuity and progression in the provision of your subject's curriculum achieved?
- How is assessment carried out and progress recorded?
- How does your subject contribute towards the development of the key skills of oracy, literacy, numeracy and information technology?
- How does it contribute to the development of pupils' attitudes and their spiritual, moral, social and cultural development?

Teaching:
- How well is your subject taught?
- What strengths and weaknesses in the teaching of your subject are you aware of?

Resources and staffing:
- How well is your subject resourced?
- What effect does the level of resources have on the provision and quality in your subject? How are resource needs identified and met?
- How do you work to develop staff expertise in your subject?
- What INSET have you attended? What INSET have you led?
- What INSET have other staff attended and how is information shared?

Management and leadership:
- How does your subject feature in the school's development planning process?
- What steps do you take to monitor and evaluate all aspects of the provision for, and outcomes of, your subject?
- How are you supported in doing your job?
- How and by whom is your performance in your role monitored?

FIG 5.1b
Coordinator interview questions

1 Brief description of your background, qualifications, training and experience.

2 Brief description of your role in the school as coordinator: including if applicable — ongoing advice and support to colleagues; gathering information and research reports; providing subject specialist teaching; monitoring policy implementation and use of schemes of work; modelling good teaching in the subject; developing assessment techniques; moderating work through the collection of samples; developing teaching approaches; evaluation of coverage.

3 Who is responsible for the quality of teaching the subject in this school? Who is responsible for the standards of children's work; children's progress in the subject? What has been done so far to raise standards?

4 How was the policy arrived at; what planning processes are usual; how do you know all staff are doing it; how will you evaluate the effectiveness of your programme; what do you expect the result to be — on achievement; on progress; on teachers' levels of understanding?

5 How do you influence other teachers' teaching? How do you ensure a continuous programme between classes; between KS1 and KS2 and progression of knowledge and skills? How do you get an overview of standards? Do you have non-contact time to fulfil this role?

6 Do you have a role in monitoring teachers' plans, pupils' work? What actually happens? What arrangements are made for children with special needs in your subject?

7 How are resources for the subject managed? Budget, audit; organisation; ordering; replenishment; distribution; emergencies.

8 What subject INSET has been provided; how were INSET needs identified? What has been provided in school; in other institutions; have you led any sessions?

9 Please comment on any links with the community; other schools; use of the environment?

10 What are your aims for development of the school's subject curriculum? How will you know if you have achieved them? What needs doing next?

11 How do you record children's progress in the subject and report it to parents?

Subject summary forms

Subject inspectors have to complete a subject summary form rating from 1 (excellent) to 7 (poor) for each of the following aspects. As a coordinator preparing for inspection you might usefully consider each category and give your own score in your subject. What comment might you make to justify or explain the score you have given?

Grade 1 Excellent
Grade 2 Very good   Favourable   Well above average   promotes very high standards and quality
Grade 3 Good
Grade 4 Satisfactory   Broadly Typical   Average   promotes sound standards and quality
Grade 5 Unsatisfactory
Grade 6 Poor   Unfavourable   Well below average   promotes low standards and quality
Grade 7 Very poor

	KS1	KS2	Overall	Your comment
EDUCATIONAL STANDARDS ACHIEVED				
Attainment				
Progress				
Progress of pupils with SEN				
Attitude, behaviour and personal development				
QUALITY of EDUCATION				
Teaching				
The Curriculum				
Assessment				
MANAGEMENT and EFFICIENCY				
Leadership and Management				
Staffing accommodation and learning resources				
Efficiency				

Components of teaching	KS1	KS2	Your comment
Teachers' knowledge and understanding			
Teachers' expectations			
Teachers' planning			
Methods and organisation of teaching			
Management of pupils			
Use of time and resources			
Quality and use of day to day assessment			
Use of homework			

Components of judgments about the curriculum	KS1	KS2	Your comment
Breadth and balance of the subject curriculum			
Equality of access and opportunity			
Provision for pupils with SEN			
Planning for progression and continuity			

Components of judgments about assessment	KS1	KS2	Your comment
Procedures for assessing pupils' attainment			
Use of assessments to inform curriculum planning			

	Overall	Your comment
Comtribution of IT to pupils' SMSC Development		

Components of judgments about leadership and management	Overall	Your comment
Leadership: clear educational direction for the subject in the school		
Support and monitoring of teaching and curriculum development in the subject		
Development planning, monitoring and evaluation		
The ethos for learning		

Components of staffing, accommodation and learning resources	Overall	Your comment
Match of number, qualifications and experience of teachers to the demands of the curriculum		
Match of number, qualifications and experience of support staff to the demands of the curriculum		
Arrangements for the professional development of staff		
Adequacy of accommodation for the effective teaching of the subject		
Adequacy of resources for effective teaching of the subject		

Components of efficiency	Overall	Your comment
Use of teaching and support staff		
Use of learning resources and accommodation		

Is there recorded evidence of significant variations in any of the following?	Yes or No	Your comment
Attainment or progress of girls and boys?		
Attainment or progress of different ethnic groups?		
Overall attainment over time?		
Progress of pupils of differing attainment?		
Is there non-compliance with the National Curriculum?		
Is there non-compliance with Health and Safety requirements?		

(adapted from the subject profile which is reproduced with the kind permission of OFSTED)

What a subject coordinator needs to do in order to address the issues covered above and to achieve high quality and thus be in a strong position to meet the challenges of the inspection process in general and the interview in particular, forms the substance of Parts 3 and 4 of the handbook. They are concerned with how you will be able to develop quality in your subject and how to monitor and evaluate the effects of the structures and processes which you have contributed to putting in place. You should be in a position to know where you are up to as a coordinator and have clear plans for the future development of your subject and your role in developing it.

National reports by HMCI and HMI frequently cite aspects of the teaching process which are associated with high, or alternatively low, standards of achievement. This has always been the case. In 1876 one HMI wrote

 I regret to say worse results than ever have been obtained. The failures are almost invariably traceable to radically imperfect teaching. (Cockcroft, 1982)

More recently a study into the teaching of number in primary schools *The Teaching of Number in Three Inner-urban LEAs* (OFSTED, 1997b), looks at the quality of teaching and pupils' achievement in classes for Year 2 (6 and 7-year-olds) and Year 6 (10 and 11-year-olds) in the three metropolitan boroughs. The report commends the excellent teaching found in some schools, but calls for urgent attention to be given to the fact that variations in the quality of teaching and, therefore, the achievement of pupils across each authority are unacceptably wide.

The report found that the best lessons featured essential elements, such as:

- clarity of teachers' explanations and instructions;
- teachers' ability to ask the right questions and promote comprehension and confidence in using mathematical language;
- an insistence that pupils know basic number facts and tables by heart;
- effective assessment and feedback of pupils' weaknesses in order to target areas for improvement;
- skill in relating new work to what has been taught previously.

Some teaching, however, was found to be '*confused and confusing, leading to poor attitudes, if not anxieties, about number in many pupils.*'

HMI also found significant variations in the quality of classroom management. The best lessons usually had more time spent on teaching the class together, with individual and group work closely linked to whole class. These are consistent themes and because the quality of teaching is of central importance in the inspection process, coordinators will need to consider in more detail the criteria against which it will be judged by the inspection team. The criteria apply to all subjects and the educational provision for children under five, and so are of relevance to all coordinators.

Section 5.1 of the OFSTED framework and guidance handbook are concerned with teaching. Inspectors have to evaluate and report on the quality of teaching they observe with reference to the contribution it makes to the levels of pupils' attainment and the progress they are making in their learning. It is worth noting here that the whole of the inspection is focused on the outcomes of the education process in terms of the effect of all the school's work on pupil achievement. It is outcome driven and everything is to a large extent judged on how it contributes to standards of learning and behaviour and the progress and development of pupils.

Inspection Report

In the good and excellent lessons teachers prepare well. They provide their pupils with plenty of opportunities to develop speaking and listening skills, present stimulating materials and engage and challenge pupils with ideas and encourage thoughtful responses. These teachers are secure in their understanding pupil's needs and the learning objectives of the curriculum. An example seen during the inspection was the Lowry topic in Year 3 where children developed an understanding of the artist and his approach through dressing up and photographing each other in groups against a backdrop of old Salford scenery created by other children in the class. In such lessons children are excited to learn and rapidly develop a range of inter-related skills

Church school — March 1997

In reporting on the quality of teaching, inspectors have to point out the overall strengths and weaknesses of the teaching, in relation to teaching of children under five, the pupils in each of Key Stages 1 and 2 and in the different subjects and areas of learning they inspect. They have to evaluate and report on factors which account for effective and ineffective teaching and the extent to which teaching promotes the learning of all pupils. Particular attention will be paid by inspectors to those pupils who have special educational needs or for whom English is an additional language.

The different elements of teaching which inspectors have to consider in coming to judgments about its quality are clearly specified in the inspection guidance handbook. They must look at the extent to which the teaching demonstrates a secure knowledge and understanding of the subject or area of learning being taught. They must judge the extent to which the teaching has high expectations of the pupils. Does it challenge pupils' thinking and deepen their knowledge and understanding of the subject matter?

Inspectors will consider the effectiveness with which the teaching is planned and prepared. Is there a clear focus for the teaching and are the activities the pupils will do and the teaching taking place targeted on achieving the objectives set out? Resources necessary to support the teaching intentions and achieve the learning outcomes should be available, prepared and accessible. The work should be adapted to meet the needs of pupils who learn at different rates. The teaching should employ methods and organisational strategies which match the curricular objectives and the needs of the range of pupils being taught. This will, the OFSTED guidance suggests, involve different forms of pupil grouping and teacher focus, on individuals and groups as well as the whole class, and a range of pedagogic skills: exposition, explanation, demonstration, discussion, practical activities, investigation, testing and problem-solving. The key to the judgments in these areas is the extent to which the organisation and methods fit the purpose of achieving high standards of work and behaviour, extends pupil knowledge and understanding and develops their skills. Inspectors will judge teaching on the extent to which it manages pupils well and achieves high standards of discipline

Inspection Report

Teaching in history varies significantly. At Key Stage 1 teaching is satisfactory. The lessons are planned to interest the pupils and there is a mix of video, talk and activity which is appropriate to the pupils' age. At Key Stage 2, the teaching is poor. The activities are not appropriate to the age of the pupils and are not used as a basis for further learning. Classroom control is frequently poor with much unchecked disruption. The activities do not interest or challenge the pupils sufficiently for them to make progress in their knowledge and understanding of Roman life. Teachers' knowledge and understanding of the National Curriculum Programme of Study for history are very weak. Teachers' plan around topic themes and the content for each unit is left to individuals. This has a negative effect on pupils' learning, since history is taught to them in isolated units often unrelated to any other aspect of their learning.

The coordinator for history has been in post for only two months and has other significant responsibilities in the school. There is no scheme of work for history and this is the major weakness contributing to low attainment in the subject. Many areas of the National Curriculum are ignored or taught superficially. There is no skills teaching in the subject. There has been no INSET for staff to improve their expertise in this subject and many rely heavily on video programmes and worksheets to support their lack of expertise. There is no assessment of the work done in history and pupils are not informed about their progress in the subject.

One form entry primary — October 1998

and the extent to which time and resources are efficiently and effectively used. Central to judgments against these criteria is how productively pupils are working and the proportion of the available time they spend concentrating on the target task of the lesson. Lessons should be brisk in pace, but there must be time for consolidation and reflection where this is appropriate.

Assessment is seen as an integral part of teaching. Therefore the quality of teaching observed will also be judged on the extent to which pupils' work is thoroughly and constructively assessed and the assessment made used to inform future teaching. The inspection of teaching quality is concerned with teachers' formative, day to day assessment. Discussion with teachers and pupils and the scrutiny of pupils' work will form part of the inspectors' evidence in addition to direct observation. Finally, inspectors must take into account the effectiveness with which homework is used to re-inforce and/or extend what is learned in school.

The direct observation of teaching by inspectors and the judgments they make are recorded to a standard format on the lesson observation form (see Figure 5.2). The aggregate of these forms provides an important part of the whole evidence base of the inspection.

Each of the four elements of the form, teaching, response, attainment and progress are judged and scored against a seven point scale where 1 is the best and 7 is the worst. Grade 4 represents an expected, average, satisfactory grading and the proportion of teaching at, above and below this grade is reported in the final report as a key indicator of the strengths and weaknesses of the school. Not surprisingly, the gradings are based upon the extent to which the aspects of teaching quality described above are in place and promoting high educational standards.

Response, as it implies, is about how pupils are reacting to the teaching they are receiving. Inspectors will be interested in their attitudes, interests and motivation, their concentration on and perseverance with their work and how well they behave. They will be looking to see if pupils can, when required and as appropriate, work independently or collaboratively and show

OBSERVATION FORM

Context of the Observation

Teaching — Grade 0–7 [ ]	Evidence and Evaluation
Response — Grade 0–7 [ ]	
Attainment — Grade 0–7 [ ]	
Progress — Grade 0–7 [ ]	
Other significant evidence	

IT	SEN	EO	SII	E2L	Rd	Wr	Sp	Li	Nu	Staffing	H/Safety	Resources	Accomm	SMSC

Uses grades 0 or 1–7 with   0 = insufficient evidence   2 = very good/well above average   4 = satisfactory/about average   6 = poor/well below average

Inspector		Teacher	

FIG 5.2
Lesson observation form

respect for others, forming and maintaining good relationships; whether they are capable of showing and taking initiative; using resources effectively and so on. Response is thus judged on the extent to which pupils behave well, utilise a range of learning strategies and show positive attitudes.

Judgments on attainment are made with reference to what pupils know, understand and can do in relation to national expectations, which will be rooted in the Programmes of Study, Attainment Targets and Level Descriptions of the National Curriculum or the Desirable Outcomes of Learning for under fives. Reference will be made, where relevant, to the attainment of pupils with special educational needs and to any differences between the attainment of different groups, for example boys and girls or ethnic groups. Gradings are made in relation to the proportion of pupils achieving above, at or below the national standards for pupils of their age.

Progress is concerned with discernible gains in skills, knowledge and understanding and evidence of what pupils learned as a result of teaching. Relevant reference will again be made to different groups of pupils, for example those with individual education plans, and the perceived ability of pupils will form the basis of judgments of the extent to which they are making the progress that might be expected of them. This will certainly include any pupils regarded as particularly able and the extent to which they are challenged and extended by the teaching.

Direct observation will also be used to gather evidence on, and come to conclusions about, the extent to which learning of the key skills in literacy, numeracy, information technology and speaking and listening are being developed and used through the different subjects. How any support staff are used, how particular lessons and activities relate to whole-school plans and how lessons contribute or are contributed to by other subjects will also be noted. It is particularly important that any support staff in the lesson, including parental volunteers, are well-briefed and clear about their roles. The situation encountered by us, where a parent was teaching phonics to a group of children in an entirely different way from the teacher (and that described in the school policy), needs to be avoided!

Inspection data

The growing data base which OFSTED and various inspection teams are gathering from the use of observation forms is beginning to highlight teaching factors which are associated with high and low standards of pupils' achievement. This is not necessarily cause and effect, but there is no doubt that there is much to be learned from the information now becoming available. Factors associated with good standards of achievement include:

- the teacher having satisfactory or good knowledge about the subject being taught;
- teachers demonstrating good questioning skills to assess pupils' learning and to challenge and extend their thinking;
- the effective use of exposition, instruction and direct teaching;
- the use of a good balance of grouping strategies, including whole class, group or individual work as appropriate;
- clear objectives for and focus of the lesson;
- good management of the time available for the lesson;
- effective use of other adults in the classroom;
- a range of techniques in the use of teacher assessment of pupils' progress;
- well-established and clearly understood classroom routines so that there is minimal disruption to teaching and learning;
- effective planning of pupils' work and good classroom organisation of resources and materials in the classroom.

There are four equally prominent teaching factors associated with lessons where standards being achieved are low:

- teachers acting as supervisors or servicers of individuals or groups of pupils, with no actual teaching being done;
- poor management and use of time in lessons, often with no deadlines being set and time being wasted at the beginnings and endings of sessions;
- an overuse of worksheets for whole classes of pupils which take no account of the range of ability and needs in the class;
- setting dull, undemanding tasks for pupils which neither challenge nor motivate them.

Other factors associated with teaching leading to low standards of achievement are an overuse of individual work; poor management and control of pupils, often linked with boring tasks; poor basic classroom organisation and management of resources; and teaching which has unclear aims and objectives which often leads to the setting of unsuitable tasks for pupils.

Clearly, the quality of teaching the inspectors find will be a major factor in their overall judgments about the quality of your subject in particular and the quality of education being provided by the school as a whole. Your knowledge of its quality, how you monitor it, support and help to improve it are potentially important parts of your role and we go on in the next chapters to look at strategies you can use to do this.

The other aspect of the inspection framework that is particularly relevant to your role is 5.2, Curriculum and Assessment. The content of the curriculum, as well as the effectiveness with which it is taught, is seen as a critical factor contributing to the educational standards reached by pupils and the progress they make in their learning. It is expected that the curriculum will be balanced and broadly based whilst meeting the statutory requirements to teach the relevant Programmes of Study of the National Curriculum in English, mathematics, IT and science. The school's own syllabus should state the extent of the curriculum in the other foundation subjects, religious education and sex education. For the curriculum of your school as a whole, at each key stage and for each subject within it, and for the areas of learning for children under five, inspectors will be looking at the extent to which it promotes pupils' intellectual, physical and personal development. The curriculum will be judged on the extent to which it provides equality of access and opportunity for all pupils to make progress. Their age, capability, gender, ethnicity and any special educational need will be taken into consideration. Provision made for pupils on your special educational needs register will be investigated to make sure that the school is meeting the requirements of the SEN Code of Practice.

The way in which the curriculum is planned is important and inspectors will look closely at this, in particular the extent to

Inspection Report

The school's mathematics curriculum is broad and balanced and during the inspection teaching was observed relating to all of the attainment targets of the National Curriculum Programme of Study. A commercial scheme is used effectively in conjunction with other materials. Whilst all pupils are given the opportunity to use a calculator, information technology is not used adequately to support pupils' mathematical learning. The school recognises the need to give more attention to the use of mental strategies, to handling data and to the practical applications of mathematics both within the subject itself and across other subjects.

Church primary school — 1997

Inspection Report

The school does not have a published overall curriculum framework or subject schemes of work which can guide teachers' termly and weekly planning. This results in the full range of National Curriculum requirements in every subject not being met and planning for continuity and progression in pupils' learning being unsatisfactory. It is not possible to ensure that the curriculum provided is built on year by year in a way which enables pupils to gain consistently in knowledge, skills and understanding as they move through the school. The school has a phased programme for putting subject schemes of work in place, which is detailed in the school development plan.

Large primary school — 1998

which pupils experience continuity and progression in their learning experiences through the teaching provided by your curriculum. The inspection will want to establish the extent to which effective processes for assessing pupils' progress through the curriculum and the standards they attain are used to inform future planning. And the curriculum is seen as comprising all of the school's planned activities within and beyond the timetable, so enrichment through extra-curricular provision, including sport (of particular relevance to those of you who are coordinators for physical education) will be inspected and reported on.

You will be keen to make sure that the curriculum for your subject meets all of the inspection criteria and we now go on, in the next section, to look at ways of developing a quality curriculum and assessment processes.

Part three Developing quality in your subject

Chapter 6
Curriculum policy and policy formation

Chapter 7
Resource management and staff development

Curriculum policy and policy formation

> ❝ *If a policy document exists then you have a starting point to compare practice and policy and something to guide discussions with staff. If not, or if the policy bears no relation to reality, then sooner or later you will need to begin the process of working with your teacher colleagues to create one which does.*
>
> Mike Harrison in *Coordinating ICT across the Primary School* (1998)

The previous section indicated that the inspection team will look at any policy documentation, schemes of work, curriculum plans, guidelines and so on relevant to the various subject areas. As this list indicates, there is enormous potential for the proliferation of paper. As Neville West (1995) says in his book *Middle Management in the Primary School*:

> ❝ *At present, many schools feel overwhelmed by the need to produce detailed documentation and are aware of the range of documentation which a school is invited to furnish prior to an OFSTED inspection, not the least of which are policy documents.*
>
> (p. 25)

This chapter will clarify the nature and purpose of policy and policy documentation as well as indicating how policies are devised and implemented to give them the best chance of being successful. And let us be clear, as far as OFSTED are concerned, success for a policy can only be measured by the quality of education it supports, the progress the pupils make in their learning and the standards they achieve in their work. West goes on to say, quite rightly, that all schools have policies even when there is nothing written down. They rely on implicit policy made up of shared assumptions and tacit understandings underpinned by custom and norms of practice. And in terms of the criteria that the end of policy is quality, progress and high standards, it is possible for these to be achieved in schools where there is no written policy. Conversely, there will be schools with comprehensive and immaculately produced policy documentation which appears to have no reflection in the school's practice and is not leading to good quality provision and appropriate levels of achievement. However, in a time of change and accountability, it seems sensible that the position a school should be seeking is to have clear, concise written policies which reflect and are reflected by the practice in the school.

The nature and purpose of the policy

It is important to understand from the outset that a policy is not a piece of paper! It is a set of behaviours and transactions, the things you do in your school and how you do them. In this sense, a policy is an agreement which all members of staff have entered into. All should follow the policy. No-one really has a right not to follow school policy, even if he or she disagrees with it, until such time as it is changed or modified through the school's processes for doing so. If this is the case, then the way in which the policy is developed is important. The theory is that if people have been involved in the formation of policy then they will have a stake in it and be more likely to adhere to it. Experience suggests that although by no means certain, this assumption that 'ownership' will increase the likelihood of commitment is in fact quite often borne out. It is therefore important to consider the process of policy making and how as many people as possible are to be relevantly involved. When we come to consider why policy making can fail, it is often the case that the people who are supposed to implement the policy were not in general those who articulated the issues the policy was to address nor were they involved in the formulation of the policy. One of the difficulties of successful policy implementation in schools is that changes in circumstances, issues and people occur, sometimes all too frequently. New staff will not by definition

Key reasons for having a policy document include:

- to guide lesson planning;
- to inform teachers and pupils what is expected of them;
- to identify resource needs; and,
- to inform INSET planning.

Harrison (1998)

have been involved in the initial policy making process. There must be mechanisms for inducting staff into policy procedures and for policy to be re-visited as often as is practicable. Formal and informal opportunities exist to achieve this and are considered below.

It is important in policy-making that we don't take action until we are conceptually clear about what we are trying to do. What is policy compared with, say, a scheme of work? Where do guidelines fit in? We must be very careful that we do not reach a situation where the production of documents takes precedence over their purpose! This will lead to implementation overload, token adoption, repetition, ambiguity and confusion. So, if we agree that policy has to be adhered to by everyone in the school, it is important that we are clear about where school policy ends and flexibility for individuals begins. How prescriptive a policy is depends upon what has been agreed. Policy, that which has been agreed to be carried out by everyone, can be anywhere on a continuum from one that is very detailed in what is required to be taught, how, when and so on, to one in which there is maximum choice for the individual teacher. To some extent this can be seen as blurring the distinction between policy, scheme of work, guidelines. If a detailed scheme of work which indicates content, methodology, timing, lays down who is to teach what, when and how then it is clearly policy. But if the scheme of work just makes suggestions of a range of things you might do to fulfil broad learning objectives, with ideas about how to do them and the individual can choose the what and the how and the when, it will be advice, guidance and support rather than policy.

A whole school policy can:
- publicly demonstrate the school's intentions for children's learning within the subject;
- help make a case for funding;
- give information to parents, governors and inspectors;
- provide a framework for individual teacher's planning;
- aid coherence, continuity, progression and shape priorities;
- assist in achieving uniformity and consistency in school decision making by helping to focus the minds of various decision making groups such as governors, the senior management team, other subject coordinators, toward common aims.

Schools clearly differ in the extent to which there is prescription for everyone or choice for individuals. An important element of successful policy making is to ensure clarity about what is prescribed and what is not. As an individual coordinator you will be operating in a particular school culture in this regard, which may very well result from the leadership or management style of the headteacher. The effect you can have will be variable in terms of the policy debate. However, you need to be clear about where you stand. And indeed, in an OFSTED inspection, it is important that you and your colleagues are singing with more or less the same voice on such issues. Confusion or disagreement about what constitutes policy is not a strong position from which to undergo such rigorous external accountability. There is no doubt that the culture of relationships in your school will have an important effect on the effectiveness of your policy-making processes and policy implementation. In an ideal world there will be a recognition that good professional relationships need to be fostered. They will depend upon:

- the open, honest discussion of educational ideas, aims and methods;
- the active co-operation of colleagues with each other in sharing ideas, resources and in helping each other to develop skills, knowledge and expertise;
- valuing each other's contributions as a staff team;
- having consideration for other colleagues and not allowing personal feelings to colour professional judgments;
- individuals adhering to agreed school policies and procedures and taking active steps to develop professionally in order to contribute to the development of the whole school.

You will know, and perhaps will already have identified in your completion of Activity 2 in Chapter 2, the extent to which these attitudes exist in your school. As a coordinator, you will want to act in the above ways personally and try to influence others no matter what the overall ethos of your situation is. That is something over which you will have control.

The policy for your subject or area, will be constructed within a wider framework as shown in Figure 6.1.

FIG 6.1

A school framework for curriculum policy development

National policy imperatives:
The National Curriculum; The National Inspection Schedule; National Targets for Literacy and Numeracy.

Local policy initiatives:
LEA education development plan; LEA statement on the school curriculum as adopted or adapted by your school;

Your school's philosophy and aims:
school curriculum statements, aims and objectives; a whole school policy for approaches to teaching and learning may flow from this;

The school development plan:
setting the agenda for curriculum review, development and monitoring: prioritisation and resource implications;

School policies for specific subjects and aspects:
in line with overall school aims and teaching-learning philosophy/policy;

Implementation of curriculum policy:
this will be through a detailed scheme of work, which may be a clear paradigm for each subject, describing how continuity and progression in the subject is achieved, or through the long- and medium-term planning framework of the school;

Detailed teaching and learning of the curriculum:
teachers' short-term planning, which will incorporate assessment and differentiation as well as the necessary arrangements for managing and resourcing the learning;

The quality of teaching and learning in the classroom:
the *raison d'etre* of the whole process, which must be monitored, evaluated and reviewed regularly and systematically.

Good arts teaching is of lasting benefit for all pupils. Contact with the arts enriches pupils' lives and helps them acquire worthwhile knowledge and skills, including an ability to question, explore ideas, appreciate and strive for a high quality of performance. These are the findings of OFSTED in a report: 'The Arts Inspected: Good Teaching in Art, Dance, Drama and Music'.

'The work amply illustrates the benefit of a rich arts curriculum for all pupils and the commitment of teachers to achieving high standards', says Jim Rose, HMI.

The background to the report were the 10,000 school inspections carried out in 1995/6 and '96/7. OFSTED also intends to produce an appendix to this report that will be on OFSTED's web site, http://www.ofsted.gov.uk. The report is available from Heinemann Educational, PO Box 380, Oxford OX2 8BR.

OFSTED press release

Your familiarity with the elements outlined in Figure 6.1 will come partly from the ways in which you have used reading as outlined in Chapter 3 and partly to do with the ways in which your own school communicates its philosophy, structures and processes to all members of the school team.

Before moving on to look at the actual mechanisms you might operate to construct and implement policies, we look at what might be conceived as the difference between a curriculum policy and a scheme of work, bearing in mind our discussion at the beginning of this chapter, and that the implementation of schemes may be part of policy.

A curriculum policy is a documented statement which sets out the general framework and overall approach to a subject or area of learning experience, reflecting the school's beliefs and intentions and in line with the overall framework specified above. The following areas may well be included in your curriculum policy document:

- a statement which indicates the unique elements of the subject or area of study;
- curriculum aims specific to the subject or study area;
- links to National Curriculum Programmes of Study where this is appropriate;
- ways in which curriculum activities will be planned;
- the principles and methods by which the subject will be taught;
- how continuity and progression in the teaching and learning of the subject is to be achieved;
- how teaching in the subject will be differentiated to meet the range of needs and abilities of pupils to whom the curriculum will apply, including those with special educational needs;
- procedures for assessment and record-keeping in the subject or area:
- procedures for the use of resources and equipment;
- how equal opportunities will be guaranteed for all pupils;
- the roles of people with management responsibility within the policy; and,
- the ways in which the implementation and success of the policy will be monitored, evaluated and reviewed.

All but the first three points in this list may be unnecessary if your school has a generic teaching and learning policy which specifies how these aspects will be dealt with for all subjects. To include them if this is the case would clearly be repetitive and lead to that proliferation of paper which was referred to earlier. Essentially, policy is saying what your subject in your school is all about and what are the important principles on which we base the teaching and learning of it. As you can see, it is likely to be similar for all subjects or areas. A skeleton generic policy document can be found in *Developing a*

Leadership Role in the Key Stage 2 Curriculum (Harrison, 1995) and subject specific books in this series.

The scheme of work is subject based. In the first place it identifies which parts of the curriculum, and that for most subjects will mean which parts of the National Curriculum, should be taught to each class or year group. It's about how your school will divide up the curriculum so that teachers know what to teach and thus can achieve continuity in the curriculum, avoiding unplanned repetition. It provides a map for whole school progression in the subject and is, in effect, the school's long-term curriculum plan.

The scheme of work must then enable teachers to draw down from their allotted curriculum in order to be able to ask and answer the following question. What is it specifically that I want my pupils to learn? These are often referred to as learning objectives or learning outcomes. A good way of clarifying this will be to ask what is it that I want them to know, or understand or be able to do which they can't do now? The scheme of work should set out these outcomes very clearly, and then go on to identify the teaching activities that are likely to lead to the desired learning taking place. Teachers will then be helped, through the scheme of work, to answer the question, how will I find out if the desired learning has taken place, that the learning objectives have been achieved? In other words, we are now talking about assessment, and often assessment needs good subject knowledge if pupil's learning behaviour is to be recognised and understood. The scheme of work can be critical in providing the subject information necessary if non-specialists are to implement curriculum policy and the scheme of work effectively. This part of the scheme is the school's medium-term planning.

Given the support of a clear policy and detailed scheme of work, short-term planning then becomes the individual teacher's adjustments as the work of implementing the scheme/medium-term plan gets underway. It is about how pupils get on with previous activities, whether they need more work, or can proceed more quickly; it's about whether particular groups or individuals need more help or greater challenge. This is almost certainly not part of any scheme of

---

Inspection Report

The school has policy statements for all subjects of the National Curriculum and RE. These are consistent in presentation, layout and content and are reviewed regularly. They help to ensure that the National Curriculum is covered in a progressive way, providing useful advice to teachers as they plan their lessons, and allowing good practice to be shared. A recently adopted health education policy is extending the general curriculum.

Staff planning for pupils' work is very good. All teachers produce written plans and half-termly evaluations. Most of these are of high quality. Governors are consulted in policy making and are involved in monitoring through their scrutiny of regular reports for the headteacher and other members of staff. The contribution of nursery nurses and non-teaching assistants in planning is very effective.

Homework arrangements have a positive influence on the quality of learning. There are effective procedures for assessment, recording and reporting.

Large primary school — 1996

work, it hardly can be, and is about the professionalism of individual teachers as they match their implementation of your subject policy and scheme to ensure that individual pupils make the best possible progress.

As you will infer from what we have said about schemes of work, they are very closely connected with curriculum planning, at the long-term and most particularly at the medium-term. If there is no actual scheme of work in place for your subject, then teachers' curriculum plans are the *de facto* scheme of work — what is actually taught in the school for your subject. Some schools have approached the task of constructing a scheme of work by analysing a year's curriculum planning at the end of the period and using this as the basis for, where necessary, re-ordering and adding to what is done in order to come up with a scheme. This is an alternative to writing a scheme and then implementing it. It is a form of action-based development, using what is already done and being done, and builds up the scheme collaboratively over time. Your task then is coordinating and supporting the work.

Developing your policy

You will know where your school is up to generally with regard to the documentation of its policies and schemes of work. Everything may be in place, nothing may be in place or you may have part of the job done. Reference back to the previous activities you have carried out in the handbook should clarify this. The processes whereby policy and schemes of work are developed will vary, but frequently coordinators take the lead in drafting documents that then go back to the staff in order that they can be discussed, modified and re-drafted. This may vary, with small groups or working parties working on different policies or schemes. Again, reference back to the activities carried out in Chapter 3 will be helpful in terms of the management skills and abilities you may need if you find yourself in this leadership role. How easy or difficult this role is will depend upon a number of factors, most of which we have already rehearsed and particularly those to do with professional relationships in your school.

Suggestion

Activity 13
Consider the problems and opportunities presented as you led (or are about to lead) the formulation and implementation of policy/construction of a scheme of work in your school.

Characteristics of a good policy statement:
- it has the commitment of everyone to whom it applies because they were involved in its construction and can see its value to the school and to themselves;
- it is based on clear understanding of its purposes, which themselves are focused on achieving school goals;
- it makes clear what is expected of groups and individuals within the school and why;
- it should therefore lead to planned actions and clear behaviours: what is done and the way it is done, within the agreed limits of proscription;
- it should provide a basis for the school to be able to evaluate its performance;
- it should be as brief as possible and written in a clear, jargon-free style which can be easily understood by all members of the school community.

The difficulty you experienced or anticipate experiencing may well be related to whether or not the issues involved are likely to be seen by colleagues as contentious or non-contentious. Contentious issues will be those where there is significant disagreement, conflict or dissatisfaction with current or proposed practice. Where there is agreement, and no real contention, written policy will be straightforward and may be formulated by the simple documentation of current practice. This will not always be possible. Of course, some conflict is helpful, remember when two people always agree then one of them is probably unnecessary. Where issues are contentious, or likely to be so, the following ideas may be of help:
- try to form working parties representing different points of view — don't be the only one responsible for drafting ideas;
- try to get people on the working party who have expertise, credibility and a stake in the outcomes;
- make sure the working party gets information from as wide a range of sources as possible;
- formulate more than one option for action to help build consensus;
- options should be based on real examples of good action where this is possible;
- refine all elements of consensus into a well-written statement and emphasise that review will take place as the policy/scheme is implemented, monitored and its effectiveness evaluated;

Subject:

NC year:

Time:

NC PoS reference	Suggested activity(ies)	Resources/ organisation	Learning target	Assessment information needed	Links with other subjects	Development/use of key skills

© Falmer press

FIG 6.2
Format for a scheme of work

- policy making and implementation is often an extended process: do not be anxious about the time which may be necessary to involve and consult everyone, acknowledge the needs of others, implement action plans and monitor, evaluate, review and adjust what is done; and,
- at all stages, consult with and keep informed the headteacher/senior management.

Whatever your particular circumstances and the processes and procedures you have had to go through, you will want to end up with good policies and schemes of work. The following checklist indicates what can be regarded as good quality for each of them.

Characteristics of a good scheme of work:
- it makes clear to teachers for each class exactly what they have to teach in the subject and how much time is available to teach it and links content specifically to National Curriculum Programmes of Study;
- it translates the content into clear learning objectives and activities which will lead to their achievement, these may include suggestions for links with other subjects, with cross-curricular themes and with the development and application of key skills;
- it identifies teaching approaches and resources suitable to the carrying out of the activities and their associated learning objectives;
- it is in a format that can easily be added to, modified and developed in the light of evaluation (for example a loose-leaf folder);
- it enables teachers to plan and implement high quality teaching programmes which lead to pupils following a coherent programme of work that enables them to build progressively on earlier learning.

The purpose of the scheme of work (Figure 6.2) is to translate policy into practice in a way which reflects the school's overall curriculum aims and secures balance, continuity and progression. Any documentation should support teacher's medium- and short-term planning, and may, if it is detailed and proscriptive enough, replace the medium-term. A format for presenting a scheme of work which could also be used for teachers' medium term planning is shown in Figure 6.2.

FIG 6.3
Planning and learning
assessment cycle

When you have in place a clear policy and scheme of work for your subject you are well on the way to developing a quality curriculum. What we have not mentioned so far, and as you are aware is explicitly linked with curriculum provision and the quality of teaching, is how we actually assess pupils' learning as a result of it. In the OFSTED framework assessment is part of the quality of teaching aspect and the curriculum and teaching aspect, and in both cases the emphasis is on the use of assessment to inform planning and support the further learning of pupils. Your policy and scheme of work may refer to assessment or again, in some schools it could be part of an overall teaching and learning policy or indeed a free-standing policy for assessment, recording and reporting (see Figure 6.3).

It is not possible in this handbook to go deeply into assessment issues. A brief resume of the main points to borne in mind will suffice. If you are interested in further reading on assessment, Ruth Sutton's two books, *Assessment: A Framework for Teaching* (1991) and *Assessment for Learning* (1995) are both readable and informative. She makes it quite clear that assessment is part of a cyclical process which begins with planning.

Good teacher assessment starts with planning. The more clear we are about what we want pupils to know, understand and be able to do as a result of the learning experiences, tasks and activities we give them, the easier it is to judge whether individual children have achieved the objectives. The decisions then made about whether or not the desired learning has taken place are based on a mass of information about the pupils which is coming to us all the time and in many ways. We watch, listen, question, mark work, set tests and assessment tasks, both formal and informal and in these and many other ways build up our knowledge about individual pupils and what they are achieving in the subject. This is continuous teacher assessment. We need to be clear that how we assess and how we interpret the National Curriculum assessment criteria in the level description of the attainment targets is consistent. Constant professional dialogue about this for the different subjects is critical. Useful starting points for such 'moderation' activities are the series of exemplification of standards booklets *Consistency in Teacher Assessment* published by the School Curriculum and Assessment Authority (SCAA, 1995a,b,c). These booklets cover the core subjects of English, mathematics and science and include a video for exemplifying standards in speaking and listening. More recently SCAA have produced exemplification material for National Expectations in the non-core subjects. You will need to be familiar with your own (SCAA, 1997a–g). Many schools retain a central portfolio of examples of their own pupils' work which identify the agreed standards against which teacher assessments are made. They help to achieve consistency in the assessment levels recorded on class records and those recorded and reported statutorily at the end of the key stage. They also provide evidence to external monitoring bodies of the school's systems to achieve accurate and consistent assessment standards. OFSTED's guidance handbook states:

❝ *Teachers do not need to keep detailed records to support the assessments they make of each pupil: they need only collect samples of work which exemplify attainment at each level. Inspectors should use these samples to examine the comparability of individual teacher's judgements.* (p. 79)

From the enormous amount of information thus made available about pupils' progress in learning and the standards they are achieving, decisions must be made about what we need to record, how it is to be recorded and for whom. The principles underlying decisions on these questions should be:

- is what we record really useful and in what ways;
- how much time does the recording take and what might be alternative uses for that time;
- crucially, does the information really enable decisions to be made about planning future work for children?

Recording systems have to be manageable and avoid teachers being engaged in excessively detailed, repetitive or time-consuming tasks. Figure 6.4 gives a simple individual record sheet to track pupils' progress through the National Curriculum subjects which have levels in their Attainment Targets. Art, music and physical education, which just have end of key stage statements, are not included. If the record is filled in annually against the level descriptions for each Attainment Target, it will enable year on year planning against the attainment of pupils. The teacher comment column will enable indications to be made of strengths or omissions for an individual pupil within the level description. For example, a pupil may fulfil all of the criteria for Level 3 writing except for handwriting. The column would be used to record this fact, although Level 3 would be ticked as that which is a best fit description of the work characteristically produced by the pupil. It should also be helpful as teachers come to write their annual reports on each child. Some schools may wish to complete the record more frequently, but in any case the day by day, on-going assessment of teachers as described above will lead to the summative judgments recorded.

The formal, statutory requirements for assessing and reporting pupil's progress are clearly set out in the DfEE documentation which is published annually to support end of key stage national assessment and testing procedures. If you coordinate a subject which is part of this regime, you should make yourself aware of the requirements for administration and the substance of the tests and tasks. Remember that the annual written report on individual pupils, for parents, should make clear the strengths and weaknesses of the pupil for each of the National Curriculum subjects and religious education.

The timing and nature of your work on the development of policy for your subject or area, schemes of work and planning, will to an extent be determined by the order of priorities

Primary school National Curriculum record sheet

Child's name _ _ _ _ _ _ _ _ _ _ _ _ _   Year _ _ _ _ _ _ _ _ _ _ _ _ _   Date _ _ _ _ _ _ _ _ _ _ _ _ _

National Curriculum Level

W 1 2 3 4 5 Teacher   Comment

English:
   Speaking and listening
   Reading
   Writing

Mathematics:
   Using and applying
   Number and algebra
   Shape, space and measures
   Handling data

Science:
   Experimental/investigative
   Life processes
   Materials\properties
   Physical properties

Design and Technology

Information Technology

History

Geography

Art

Music

Physical Education

Religious Education

FIG 6.4
Exemplar National Curriculum teacher assessment record

within your school's overall development plan, which as a coordinator you will, hopefully, have contributed to. Even if you have not, you should be aware of your subject's status within the plan. When it is a priority focus you may be heavily involved in policy review and development. At other times you will be in a 'maintenance' mode, keeping your subject going while others are the developmental focus.

Technically, of course, all of the school's policies are those of its governing body. This is true even when they have had little or no input into their construction and implementation. Nevertheless, OFSTED inspectors will be keen to know the governing body's processes for keeping itself informed of the school's curriculum. You may well wish to be pro-active in keeping them informed, perhaps by taking curriculum reports to their curriculum sub-committee, and having a governor designated as the one with the overview of your subject or area of responsibility, although as with other things, this may be beyond your control.

Clear policies, backed up by schemes of work and agreed planning processes are a first and critical stage in striving to ensure high quality educational provision for your subject. The successful implementation of policy depends upon a number of factors to do with resourcing, which we now go on to consider.

Chapter 7 Resource management and staff development

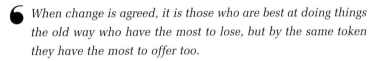

When change is agreed, it is those who are best at doing things the old way who have the most to lose, but by the same token they have the most to offer too.

Bill Tagg (1996) in *The School in an Information Age*

When you have established clear and agreed policy for your subject or area of responsibility, backed up by schemes of work and/or planning systems which support its teaching and learning, you have fulfilled a necessary condition for the achievement of quality. However, having the policy in place is one thing, its implementation in a way that fulfils its aims of providing high quality educational provision through which pupils make good progress and demonstrate high standards of achievement is another. It is not uncommon for people to react to change with anxiety, uncertainty and to suffer stress, even those who are fully committed to the change. The best laid plans of mice and men gang aft agley! Success will depend to a significant extent on the resources available to carry out the policy effectively. This will include the physical resources of books and equipment but also, and perhaps most importantly, the human resources, the skills, expertise and ability of staff to carry out the policy. We turn now to the issues around developing and maintaining quality in the areas of resource management and staff development.

Resources

The inspection of each curriculum area or subject will take account of the resources and accommodation made available for it and the extent to which teachers have the qualifications, experience and expertise to teach the subject. Judgments will be made on the extent to which accommodation, resources for learning and staffing enable the curriculum to be taught effectively to the range of pupils. Comments will be made where they constitute particular strengths and weaknesses. Evidence and judgments from individual curriculum areas and subjects are brought together and reported upon in section 6.2 of the inspection schedule: staffing, accommodation and learning resources.

If we re-visit the exemplar job description (p. 29) we see that it appears fairly straightforward with regard to the requirement to obtain and organise the physical resources, using any money made available in line with the principles of financial management spelled out in Chapter 3. However, if we consider the next requirement of the job description, which is about monitoring the effectiveness of work in the subject through the school, it is clear that we cannot regard resources as something separate, discrete. The quality of the work will be to a significant extent dependent on the resources available to carry it out. Thus we can begin to see why effective resource management has to be need based. What resources are required to service the requirements of our curriculum, our policies and schemes of work, how we do things in relation to our whole school teaching and learning policy? We can only make proper provision of resources when we are aware of what resource needs are generated and so the familiarity with the nature of the curriculum of your subject that results from your involvement with policy and scheme formation is essential.

The more we see of teaching the more it appears to be a pursuit the success of which frequently hinges on attention to detail. There can be few teachers who have not experienced the failure of an otherwise appropriate and well-planned lesson because of inadequate or ill-prepared resources. An exciting lesson on using some 11-year-old's knowledge of electrical circuits to make electronic board games dissolved

Inspection Report

Overall the range, quality and organisation of resources do not support the achievement of high standards and quality in design and technology. The recently appointed coordinator has an appropriate action plan to put into place a policy for the subject.

Extract from an OFSTED report:
One form entry primary school — 1995

into chaos because there was only one screwdriver to be shared between the twelve children who were involved! Some young children motivated to paint by an exciting visit to a farm and well organised follow-up discussion based on their field sketches were frustrated because the poor condition of their paint-brushes prevented them from producing pictures of high quality. What a shame, because often such experiences are unnecessary. Resource management is about making sure that teachers and learners have the tools to do the job and know how to use them.

If stage one in resource management is the identification of needs and it has been largely achieved through curriculum schemes and plans, stage two is the audit of existing resources available and an assessment of their capability for achieving the policy objectives of your subject. Clearly, at all stages, needs-based resource management involves consultation with colleagues. It can be a really good and relatively unthreatening first step in the direction of using the inter-personal skills required as you engage in monitoring and evaluation activities. So you need to carry out a systematic monitoring of resources so that an accurate inventory of what is available can be drawn up. This may, of course, involve you in poking into hidden corners of classrooms, where scarce and hard won books and equipment are jealously guarded by she who has occupied the space since time immemorial!

There is no blueprint for carrying out a resource audit. It can be time-consuming as well as having the potential for bringing you into conflict with the kind of vested interest described, the result, perhaps, of the natural acquisitiveness and hoarding tendency of many of us. Some kind of grid, as exemplified in Figure 7.1 is probably the best way to proceed.

When this task has been completed for your subject as fully as possible a number of issues may well have arisen. Because as well as identifying gaps in provision, which you will have to plan to fill, you are just as likely to find over-provision, inappropriate provision and duplication. It has not been unusual in many schools in the past for teachers to be given an annual sum of money to buy things for their classrooms, often with little direction and no monitoring. This freedom of choice

Change involves an uneasy balance between conflict and consensus, between moving too fast and too slow, between taking people with you or leaving them behind stranded and antagonistic.

Weiner (1985)

Description of item	Quantity	Location	Usage	Age condition	Date checked

FIG 7.1
Resource audit and inventory sheet

From their infancy they (the working men) had been trained to distrust their own intelligence, and to leave the management of the affairs of the world — and for that matter the next one too — to their betters, and now most of them were absolutely incapable of thinking of any abstract subject whatever. Nearly all of their betters were unanimous in agreeing that the present system was a very good one and that it is impossible to alter or improve it.

The Ragged Trousered Philanthropists (Tressell, 1905)

has led to some bizarre purchases, such as the 120 kazoos discovered at the back of a teacher's classroom cupboard soon after he retired! The belief that resources are 'ours' and go with us when we move, is the explanation for the existence of advanced dictionaries in the reception class, a legacy of the time the deputy head moved from teaching Year 6 to the under-fives for professional development! And it is notoriously difficult to get some people to give up things, even when it is clear that they are inappropriate and therefore never used. There are many stories of new broom headteachers hiring skips to dispose of old and unwanted resources only to find that items have mysteriously re-appeared in classrooms.

Again, your ability to persuade people that resources are unsuitable will depend upon issues of status as well as your powers of persuasion and argument, and you may well need the support of senior management in the debate. However, what you can do is to be clear about your reasons for wishing to dispose of unwanted resources. A good maxim to start with is 'we need to give quality to get quality'. If resources are old, dirty or broken they are no good. Neither children nor teachers should be expected to work with them. No compromise.

Resources, books or charts, especially those which give wrong or outdated information, have to go. It is still possible to find atlases in schools in which half of Africa remains coloured pink as if the winds of change had not blown away our colonial past. And be alert, also, to material which offends the substance or spirit of equal opportunities legislation by portraying stereotypical images of women or racial groups.

Once you have a clear picture of what is available to support your policy and curriculum and how it is currently used, you will be aware of where there are gaps. (You may also have identified training needs in terms of how resources are used, a point we pick up in due course.) The identification of what you need in order to fill them should be prioritised as far as possible, probably through consultation with senior management and other colleagues. You will then be into the area of resource acquisition. The actual mechanisms for spending decisions to be made varies between schools. Some schools allocate sums to each subject, others have 'bidding' systems; all should make spending plans in line with their developmental priorities. Your personal situation will have been identified in the earlier analysis of your role in the school. In any case you are likely to be relied upon to make choices on what to buy, or at least to give advice for resources within your own area of responsibility.

Almost inevitably you will find yourself in the position of not having enough money for everything you need, let alone what you want! In a situation of scarce resources it is doubly important that money is not wasted. That is why the prioritisation of need must be against the clear criteria of meeting planned curriculum objectives. Then it is a case of making yourself informed. Obviously you will use brochures and catalogues of commercial suppliers and you may well use their inspection services and demonstrations by their representatives if available. We guess the appropriate advice is, be as careful and sceptical and cost-conscious as if you were buying double-glazing for your own house. Remember that sales people are on commission, they need to sell and some are very good at it. This is excellent so long as the criteria of fitness for your curriculum purposes and order of spending priority are met. It remains the case that schools are filled with attractively presented but less than useful books and resources that someone fell for without due analysis of their worth. A bargain ain't a bargain if you don't need it. So before you embark upon purchasing, be absolutely clear about what you want and why. Resources can then be evaluated against this as you also take account of their relative cost. Chapter 3 has already dealt with some general issues of financial management and budget control. Reference back to the expenditure control and monitoring charts might now be useful (see pages 55–8).

Whatever the extent of your resources, books and equipment, if they are to be used as efficiently and effectively as possible they must be well maintained and a clear inventory kept.

Some resources may be stored centrally, some may be in classrooms. Whatever the case, the important principles are that everyone should know what is available, what it is for, how it is used, how to get hold of it and the procedures for maintaining it in good condition and returning or replacing it so that others can use it. Not much different from what well-organised teachers expect of their children.

As coordinator you will also wish to keep yourself informed about what is available through organisations, contacts and networks beyond the school.

Be aware of what is offered by local museums and art galleries. They often go beyond passive displays and provide all kinds of hands-on experiences, simulation days, historical role-plays for children which enrich and invigorate the curriculum enormously. Do you know good local field-sites for geography? What do stately homes offer? Have you explored the attitudes of local business and commercial enterprises towards becoming involved? Many schools have run successful mini-enterprises supported by many companies which have made enormous contributions to learning in a range of subjects. Other schools may have things to offer. One of your authors was once involved in a very productive link between an inner city school and a rural village school. Mutual visits for a variety of purposes achieved real educational outcomes. The potential range of such ideas and avenues is enormous. Be pro-active and keep your colleagues informed.

Figures 7.2 and 7.3 demonstrate useful ways of keeping an audit of resources in your school.

Staff development and training

We look now at issues of staff development and training, which will include point 7 in the checklist, (Figure 7.3) picking up on point 8 when we consider your monitoring and evaluation role in more detail later. As with physical resources, materials and equipment, the starting point with regard to human resources will be an audit of existing strengths and needs. And this audit also will be related to the needs of the policies and schemes in your subject.

It is useful to consider staff development in your subject under three broad headings, although of course there are clear relationships between them:

Resources for Learning Inventory		
Resource	Key purpose	Where stored/access

FIG 7.2
Learning resources inventory

Check-list for resource management			
Task	Started	Finished	Comments
Audit current provision			
Audit current usage			
Dispense with anything unsuitable			
Identify and prioritise needs in relation to curriculum objectives			
Acquire necessary resources against suitability criteria and in line with budget provision			
Establish effective maintenance, provision and control procedures			
Establish awareness of resources for learning provided by establishments/organisations beyond the school			
Ensure staff are trained to use resources in order to achieve maximum benefit to children' learning			
Monitor and evaluate the effectiveness in terms of children's progress in learning and standards achieved			

© Falmer Press

FIG 7.3
Check-list for resource management

- subject knowledge, related to the teaching skills of planning, exposition and explanation, questioning, organisation and methodology;
- assessment of pupils' learning, progress and attainment;
- the effective use of books, materials and equipment.

It must be an axiom of good management systems within a primary school that senior management and pre-eminently the headteacher, must be responsible for voicing concerns or criticisms of individual teachers, and for disciplinary action if it should be necessary. It would be wrong to expect subject coordinators to do so. This is a different matter from that of using your expertise and inter-personal skills to identify individual's needs and support colleagues in meeting them. For each need, identify the relevant training required and potential sources for the training: external INSET, formal in-house INSET, informal support and discussion, reference to the senior management team. In particular, identify where there are strengths and expertise within your school. How can they be used to support you as you seek to get the best possible provision in your area of responsibility? Access to records of colleague's qualification, training and previous responsibilities might be of help, if they are available.

Unless you are part of the senior management team of your school it may not be possible to have a great deal of effect on the performance of others, but at least you will be in a strong position, following such a systematic review, to give appropriate advice about needs and prioritisation. Ultimately, any resource management can only be judged on the basis of the art of the possible: getting the best you can from what you've got, knowing what you need and meeting needs efficiently and effectively when the opportunity arises. Training and development are very much about getting the best from people.

It is also about getting the most effective possible training provision, when training is seen as the solution to needs. This can be quite a bewildering process currently, with the proliferation of many organisations and individuals in the market for training. Most local education authorities continue to provide in-service training through their advisory and

Inspection Report

At Key Stage 2 (in science)... the majority of (teaching) is good... Teachers' own subject knowledge is satisfactory although less confident with regard to experimental and investigative principles.

Primary School, 1997

Suggestion

Activity 14
For each of the headings at the top of the page, note any current strengths and weaknesses you know of in your subject, before or after the kinds of monitoring activities described in the next chapter of the handbook. This may well involve you in identifying individuals, so there is clear potential for sensitivity. Handle carefully.

advisory teacher support services. Often, nowadays, these are offered on a business arm basis, with service level agreements with schools about what a particular level of 'buy-back' will include. There can be various levels, for example 'gold, silver or bronze' in some authorities — more time, more support, more documentation the more you are prepared to pay. The first implication for you, of course, is to know what exactly is on offer at the different levels. This can then be matched to your school's needs, which should be prioritised in your school's development plan, and to the amount of money you have available. Hopefully, in a well-managed school, there will be some connection between the two.

Another major provider of INSET are the institutions of higher education, which are now mostly university departments of education. Most of them circulate details of their training courses, conferences, seminars etc. as well as courses carrying further qualifications, to schools and LEAs. In any case, a 'phone call to the appropriate office will secure details for you — the universities too, are budget-driven and in the business of selling their expertise.

Communication

Recently, there has been an increasing number of private training and consultancy organisations, of various sizes, which offer a wide range of training opportunities. They also send circulars to schools as well as advertising in the educational press.

The existence of a good school system for communicating information about in-service opportunities is helpful. In its absence in your school there is no reason why you shouldn't institute your own, for example an INSET notice-board, a small staffroom library of books, periodicals, catalogues related to your subject — all keeping it high profile and demonstrating your enthusiasm for and commitment to it. As with all aspects of your role, the induction of new members of staff into this kind of facility, making them aware of what is on offer, perhaps especially newly qualified colleagues, is important.

Whichever source of training you use, it is important that it is of high quality and meets your requirements. It is not always easy to fulfil these criteria and many of us have attended training events after which we have rued the expenditure of precious time and money on something that was inappropriate or downright bad. Do what research you can, clarify with providers exactly what they are aiming to achieve and very importantly, have a rigorous evaluation system.

The following format should enable you both to keep track of INSET attended in your subject or area of responsibility as well as forming an evaluative checklist of quality and usefulness. The relationship between cost and evaluation should enable some simple kind of cost-benefit analysis to be undertaken. Records such as these should be kept in your coordinator's file.

Courses undertaken in (subject) year:	
Names of teacher(s) attending	Course title ....
Date; time; venue....................................	Course provider....................................
Course tutor/s....................................	Cost GEST (information)
Evaluation 	

It is also important, of course, that what people do gain from attending courses of in-service education and training is used as effectively as possible. If the evaluations are positive, then mechanisms for feedback through your normal patterns of meetings and in-house INSET activities should be used. If opportunities are available, the most effective dissemination of ideas and expertise can be through teachers working alongside each other. This depends upon some non-contact time, of course, but where it is possible and attempted, it should be evaluated against clear criteria for success. If you have advisory teachers and/or consultants working in your school, teaching and working alongside teachers, they too should be the subject of cost-effectiveness evaluation, where cost is seen in terms both of money and time — and outcomes in terms of enhanced pupil achievement.

With policy and schemes of work in place and fully documented, with necessary resources available and systems for training colleagues in the implementation of the curriculum for your area, you have done as much as you can to optimise the quality of what your school provides. The next question, which we now go on to consider, is how effective have your efforts been?

Development follow-up to **INSERVICE** activity
Focus of activity date _____ / _____ / _____
Evaluation
How will I use this in my teaching/leadership role?
Sharing with colleagues   who   what   where   when   how?
Skills and attributes gained

Part four

Monitoring your subject or area

Chapter 8
Monitoring and evaluation

Chapter 9
Action planning and
setting targets

> ❢ *As the policy had been developed with full agreement of the*
> *staff, there was an expectation that classroom practice would*
> *reflect this. There was therefore no excuse for poor teaching.*
>
> *Accepting the Blame* — Fiona Pay (1998),
> Headteacher, Ranelagh School, Ipswich

Your subject area now has clear policies, guidelines and
schemes of work in place. Teachers use these to plan their work
with the pupils. Their subject knowledge has been supported
through meetings and INSET of various kinds, and there are
sufficient resources as well as suitable accommodation to
support the achievement of curriculum plans. As a coordinator
you have worked very hard, with your colleagues, to achieve
this position. Nevertheless, the question remains, is it all going
to work? And what does 'working' mean in this context? And
so we have to consider that part of your coordinating role
concerned with monitoring and evaluation, in many ways the
most difficult and contentious. The extent to which your
school supports you in your role, through the interest of the
senior management team, provision of quality meeting time,
the provision of some non-contact time (a rare treat in most
primary schools still) and encouragement and support for your
own professional development will of course vary, as you know
from previous audit activities suggested in the handbook.

How do you monitor? If there are established systems within
your school then adopting, or adapting aspects of this will

System	Example	Strengths	Weaknesses as suggested by OFSTED (1998)
The checklist approach	*Keeping the school under review* (ILEA, 1980)	The list consist of questions pertinent to the school (or the LEA) and means that they have been agreed by staff in advance and are therefore likely to be of a less contentious nature. Thus a coordinator without seniority would be likely to be able to carry them out.	The questions seldom focus on the quality of teaching or learning, nor about solid evidence such as the standards attained by pupils over time. These are seldom used more than once so trends are not shown up.
The ballot approach	Grids (the Schools Council Project)	The advantages of this system are that a number of different people, teaching and non-teaching staff, for example, have the opportunity to nominate areas of concern. Consensual result is likely to carry weight with teachers.	This approach tends to focus more on curriculum planning, systems and policies rather than the quality of classroom work.
The curriculum-led approach		A regular cyclical review of each area of the curriculum in turn means that no subject is overlooked and frequently results in a new policy, SoW etc.	Curriculum review is frequently undertaken in the context of the coverage and design of the curriculum rather than its effectiveness in raising standards.
The appraisal-led approach		Reviews which use the results of performance appraisal can focus the evaluation where it matters on the quality of teaching and learning.	Appraisal is worthless where, for example, it is superficial, tolerant of complacency, or is based on an uncritical and cosy relationship between the appraiser and appraisee.
The quality mark approach	Investors in People — Schools Curriculum Award	These can be a useful check on the way in which staff are valued and work together as a team to a shared purpose.	None of these awards focuses explicitly on improving teaching and learning and raising educational standards.

FIG 8.1
Evaluation systems

meet the expectations of the staff team and be less contentious. However even the best systems have shortcomings. OFSTED (1998) have detailed several types of evaluation system in *School Evaluation Matters* and these and their weaknesses are listed here (Figure 8.1).

School self-evaluation, according to OFSTED (1998) is distinct from review and must be able to:
■ take an objective look at pupils' achievements and pinpoint areas of underachievement;
■ account for results by identifying strengths and weaknesses in the quality and effectiveness of any part of the school's work, particularly teaching and learning;

■ provide information for the school improvement plan, which will in future be a vehicle for raising standards.

Perhaps the first task of monitoring therefore, is to establish whether or not the principles of policy are being implemented and the aims and objectives stated specifically by the school are, if not being fully achieved, being worked towards. If the gap between the rhetoric of documentation and the reality of what is actually going on in the school is too wide, it is difficult for inspectors not to ask awkward questions! Like, why? Or does anyone actually know the real situation? Questions which strike at the heart of the monitoring process. There is no point in trying to manage any situation which directly affects children's learning

> in a half-hearted way. If one aspect of the school's activity is perceived as being 'necessary but tedious' — tangential to the core mission — or otherwise unimportant, then the school is sending dangerous messages to its audiences.   (Holmes, 1993)

Clearly, as a coordinator you may not have a great deal of control over the school's overall approach to monitoring, and if your headteacher and senior management team are prepared to 'hope for the best' and assume all is happening as proclaimed in the mission statement and aims of the school, in its policies and prospectus, then that will be the context within which you work. So as we go through the menu of what you may be able to achieve, as ever be sanguine about your situation and do that which you are able to do as well as you can.

For OFSTED, success of a policy is pre-eminently about the extent to which it enables pupils to make progress in their learning and achieve high standards. That is how effectiveness is judged.

So if you wish to be effective in your monitoring and evaluation activities, you will be guided by these imperatives and look not only at the extent to which the policies for your subject are consistently and conscientiously implemented, but also at the outcomes being achieved as a result. This means that you will be monitoring and evaluating both processes and products. What are the ways in which this can be done?

The four most important activities by which you as subject coordinator can monitor standards in your subjects are:

■ by examining teachers' planning;
■ through scrutiny of pupils' work;
■ by analysing SAT, PANDA and other test results; and,
■ in direct classroom observation.

Each of these activities is now looked at in turn and the chapter concludes with a summary of self-inspection activities for each of the subjects of the National Curriculum and for the early years.

Examining colleagues' planning documentation

Planning will tell you the extent to which the implementation of your policies and schemes of work are contained in the teaching intentions of staff. This will include the general coverage of your subject in line with the principles of continuity and progression contained in policy. Within the detail of the planning there will be information useful to you in a number of ways: areas where coverage is not in line with policy, including gaps and omissions; elements of your subject in which planning indicates some misunderstanding and so there is a need for further support and training; the use of IT, literacy and numeracy within your subject; differentiation and the targeting of pupils with special educational needs; where and by what means assessment is planned for. As you will see, the extent to which these issues can be satisfactorily examined will be supported by the quality of the work covered in Chapter 6: the better and more explicit your policies, schemes of work and planning processes are, the easier, more targeted and more effective your monitoring of planning will be.

Monitoring, of course, inevitably leads to evaluation. There is no doubt that you will come across things during the monitoring process that are not, in your opinion, up to scratch. The big question then, is what are you to do about it? It may be possible for you to use the repertoire of management and inter-personal skills referred to in Chapter 3 to intervene and have some effect. However, it more likely that you will be involved in following up and feeding back on generic issues identified from your monitoring, areas where everyone needs help. In general, although all of your individual contextual factors — school policy, your overall management status, your personal relationships will be relevant — dealing with questions of individual's competence, or their non-adherence to policies is not the role of the coordinator but of senior management.

Looking at pupils' work

When you begin to examine the outcomes of all the policy and scheme formation, curriculum planning, resourcing, INSET and training by looking at the actual outcomes in terms of pupils' learning, what they know, understand and can do, you are really entering the realms of 'proving the pudding in the eating'! You are asking questions about what children really learn rather than what we think we teach. A monitoring sweep of the actual work pupils produce in written and pictorial form can provide a very powerful tool of monitoring and evaluation. Written work produced by a sample of pupils from reception to Year 6 in your school provides little hiding place in terms of standards and progression. Thus looking at the work pupils produce can give you a great deal of information and is certainly an important tool in your monitoring and evaluating role. Looking at the work from the range of abilities and across the school will speak volumes about the overall quality of education being provided in your subject. Incorporating work scrutiny into your monitoring practice, certainly on an annual basis, probably more often, depending upon the time you have available, will put you in a powerful position when speaking to inspectors. Ideally, to help you with obtaining the cooperation of colleagues in gaining access to pupils' work (and indeed their curriculum planning) the process should be incorporated in a whole-school policy for monitoring and evaluating the curriculum and the progress your pupils are making through it and the standards they are achieving. This itself should be a sub-set of the school's policy for teaching and learning. Again, where this is not the case, then your relationships and inter-personal skills will be called into play. However, if all coordinators recognise the value of the process, all will benefit.

What can you actually learn from scrutinising samples of pupils' work? The following *aide memoire* is based upon the four categories in the inspection observation form (see Fig. 5.2): teaching, response, attainment and progress. Clearly, all of the following information will not be available to the same extent and there will be variations due to the different ages of children and the different nature of subjects. However, information on all of the points itemised is likely to be available to a greater or lesser extent. Bear in mind, of course, that there are other indicators about pupils' work that will not be seen in their work-books, folders and daily written/graphical output. Remember displays around the school, portfolios of work samples used for assessment moderation purposes, class and school records and reports and the ephemeral information you will seek and find in other ways: role play, speaking and listening, photographs, audio and video tapes, IT disks and so on.

Teaching:

■ The extent to which the requirements of the National Curriculum in your subject are being covered and the breadth and balance between different elements of the Programme of Study. Any over or under-emphasis may be identified. General conformity with school policy.

■ The appropriateness of the content of the work set, in terms of the levels and range of skills, concepts and knowledge and its relevance and challenge. Are the expectations indicated by the work appropriate for the age and ability range of the pupils?

■ The range of methods, contexts and experiences employed in teaching.

■ The extent to which opportunities for problem-solving, communicating in different ways, research and personal study are provided.

■ Is there a logical sequence of work indicated and progression and continuity in provision, for individuals, for particular groups of pupils (e.g. the more able, those with English as an additional language, particular classes or year groups) and across the key stages?

■ The extent to which assessment takes place; the range, purpose, quality and consistent application of marking procedures.

■ The extent to which the nature and structure of the tasks provided to pupils demonstrates adequate teacher knowledge.

■ Are individual education plans and any other targets for pupils met?

■ Is homework used, and if so, how?

■ The range of resources employed, including for example the use of visits and the local environment.

Response:

■ The output of work in terms both of its quality and quantity, of its accuracy and overall presentation.

■ Are tasks completed, is there evidence of pupils showing pride in and ownership of their work?

■ Evidence of understanding of what has been taught and the transfer of skills and understandings from other areas of work.

■ Pupils engaging in estimation, problem-solving, imagination, creativity and hypothesising; in presenting things in different ways, responding to expectations and evaluating their own work.

■ The extent to which pupils are able to express beliefs, feelings and values in their work, in relation to their spiritual, moral, social and cultural development.

■ The extent to which pupils engage in collaborative work, extended work requiring sustained concentration, personal study and research. Their response to homework tasks.

Attainment:

■ What pupils know, understand and can do in relation to the National Curriculum expectations and religious education agreed syllabus and the desirable outcomes of learning for children under the age of five. This will include attainment across the targets of the curriculum for your subject or area as well as across subjects from a whole-school perspective.

■ The appropriateness of levels of attainment for different groups: ability, gender, ethnicity and background.

■ Attainment in relation to individual education plans and other targets set for pupils by the school.

■ Attainments in the key skills of literacy, numeracy and information technology as applied to your subject.

Progress:

■ How well are pupils gaining in knowledge, skills and understanding, for individuals over time, across key stages and for different groups within the school?

■ At what rates are children learning and is there too much repetition or too little re-enforcement of learning?

■ Is there real evidence of improvement in quality, quantity, mastery of skills? What are pupils learning and does this represent an appropriate challenge to the range of needs and abilities within the school?

■ Are pupils applying their learning in different situations and contexts and for a range of purposes?

Reference can be made in terms of progress to any baseline assessment information you have in your school and to the results of standardised tests, National Curriculum assessment results and records of progress. We move on now to look in more detail at what monitoring and evaluation activities you might wish to carry out in relation to the increasing amount of test and assessment data available to schools.

Analysing assessment information

We have already referred to the tendency for the OFSTED inspection process to be an increasingly outcome driven model. The work pupils produce day in and day out can perhaps be seen as the most important, the most formative and informative output of the school's policies and procedures and the quality of education it provides. However, the ostensibly more objective, 'hard' data generated by the national assessment and testing regime over recent years is now regarded as critical information for judging the progress pupils make and the effectiveness of the education provided by the school. Where such data exists for your subject, it must form an essential element of your monitoring and evaluation. OFSTED inspectors will certainly place great store by it.

OFSTED PANDAs set out in black and white school performance for self evaluation

Schools now have a full tool kit to plan for improvement, says Woodhead.

Every school in England is being urged by the Office for Standards in Education (OFSTED) to adopt a PANDA to help raise standards. The PANDA in question is black and white but that is where its resemblance to the bamboo-loving zoo favourite ends. For this package, known as Performance and Assessment report, is a unique set of information for each school to help them in the development of their plans to raise standards.

It will enable schools for the first time ever to know how they are performing not only in comparison with national averages but, more significantly, with other schools with similar characteristics.

This comprehensive set of data draws on inspection evidence, test and examination performance and teacher assessment results and sets it in the context of the school's socio-economic environment. It offers an almost complete tool kit for school self-evaluation. The 24,000 PANDAs will be updated annually.

A training package for headteachers and senior managers is also being developed by OFSTED to help them acquire the skills needed for self-evaluation.

Commenting on these developments HM Chief Inspector of Schools, Chris Woodhead, said:

 OFSTED inspection provides a rigorous external critique of school performance every few years. But schools should be

> *asking themselves questions on a more regular basis and using the answers to plan a strategy for improvement. With PANDAs and the Framework, together with recent material, such as the QCA's benchmarking data, they now have the complete tool kit to help them do that.*
>
> PANDAs have been successfully piloted in five LEAs. The pilots have enabled OFSTED to judge whether headteachers will find them helpful.
>
> OFSTED press release 19 February 1998

There are a number of ways in which you can use the information generated by assessment and testing. As well as the analysis of results data, which itself can be of various kinds and presented in various ways, the responses of pupils to tasks and their script responses to test questions can prove of value. Thus one mathematics coordinator carried out a detailed analysis of her class's end of Key Stage 2 assessment test scripts, a process which yielded much food for thought, not least in that no child had scored any marks for questions about data-handling. This led directly to a review of how this part of the Programme of Study was planned for and taught. Adjustments were made to the curriculum and results improved in this area.

When we use assessment information for monitoring and evaluating performance, there are five key questions which might underpin the process.

The first question is: how is our school currently performing? This is a fairly crude and general question, but it could well lead you to examine the broad indicators which you have. For example, what proportion of pupils in the school are achieving, at the end of a key stage, the national expectation in your subject (Level 2 for pupils at the end of Key Stage 1, Level 4 at the end of Key Stage 2). Where do you stand in relation to all primary schools, information available at Key Stage 2 from published performance tables. Where do you stand in relation to all schools in your local area, and local education authorities are increasingly furnishing schools with the data related to both Key Stages 1 and 2, presented in a

number of different ways: tables, graphs, scattergrams etc.
You will need to train yourself to understand what this
increasingly available data is actually telling you and
how it can be interpreted.

A second question, inevitably posed when even the
most general data is interrogated, is: how does our school's
performance compare with that of others? Research evidence
demonstrates fairly clearly that socio-economic factors in the
backgrounds of pupils can adversely affect their attainment
and progress in school. Although this should not and cannot
be used as an excuse for the levels pupils achieve, it is
accepted that if schools are to be compared with others, it
should be on some kind of like for like basis. This has led to
the process of benchmarking: measuring standards of actual
performance against those achieved by others with broadly
similar characteristics. Amongst groups of schools sharing
similar characteristics, the benchmark represents the standard
of performance achieved by the 'best' members of the group.
This kind of data, and we shall return to it in Chapter 9, is
regarded as the most significant as schools set themselves
targets for improvement.

A third question asks: how do our school's achievements now
compare with its previous achievements? Clearly, in order to
answer this question it is necessary to have information about
previous performance, so that progress can be measured against
some kind of baseline. From September 1998 it has been a
statutory requirement for schools to carry out assessments of
all children entering full-time education, which will usually be
in the reception class. In due course this baseline information,
described in a simple numerical measure and based on the
desirable outcomes for the six areas of learning for children
under five, will be available. In the meantime, you will have
to use such baseline information as you have (which of course
for Key Stage 2 could be results at Key Stage 1) in order to
track improvements over time indicated by assessment data.
If your school uses assessment instruments other than the end
of key stage assessment tasks, tests and teacher assessments
required statutorily, for example the optional assessment
material available from the QCA, or commercially produced

standardised tests in reading, mathematics, spelling etc. such as those published by the National Foundation for Educational Research, they too can indicate any year on year trends in measured performance of pupils in your subject.

A fourth question is: are some parts of the school more effective than others? The analysis of assessment data can lead to questions about the differences in performance between key stages, year groups or classes that may need to be investigated. This is also true as a potential response to the fifth question: are some groups of pupils doing better than others, for example do boys and girls achieve broadly similar results?

In concluding this section, it is important to acknowledge that the kind of assessment data analysis touched upon here cannot lead to definitive conclusions by itself. Its main function is to raise questions about causes that will lead to further investigation, perhaps leading on to the need for the next kind of monitoring, which is concerned with more direct involvement with the interactions of the teaching and learning process.

Direct observation of teaching and learning

Opportunities for you to engage in this kind of direct monitoring may be limited. Indeed you may not be able to do it at all. However, inspectors will, using the criteria we examined in detail in Chapter 6. If you are given the chance to see your colleagues teach — what should you look for?

How well has the lesson been prepared?
- What lesson plans does the teacher keep?
    — long term (yearly)?
    — medium term (term or half term)?
    — short term (weekly)?
    — related to numeracy/literacy?
- Are written appraisals of, say; a half term's lessons kept? — a week's?
- Is the teacher confident about his/her knowledge of the subject matter?

- Does the teacher keep a record of work achieved by individuals, groups and the class?
- Have he/she and the children access to resources providing further information?
- Are all pupils' needs identified and catered for?
- Are the aims of the lesson clear?
- Is the pupil's own knowledge used as a stimulus or source of information?
- Has the teacher anticipated:
    key questions;
    vocabulary needed;
    further work for extension activities?
- Is a balance between open and closed tasks evident?
- Is there a balance between understanding, knowing and concept development?
- Is material properly prepared?
- Have pupils been grouped for particular reasons?
- Does the lesson plan show:
    adequate differentiation;
    the relationship between this lesson and the whole series;
    a relationship to the national curriculum;
    awareness of resources; and,
    continuity of teaching and progression in learning?
- Do aspects of the lesson encourage independence from the teacher?
- Are cross-curricular skills, themes and dimensions built into the planning?

Are teaching methods appropriate?
- Were methods appropriate to suit the children, the subject matter, the availability of certain aids/resources?
- Was it evidently an approach which matched the style and natural inclination of the teacher?
- Did the chosen approach take account of the varying levels of ability in the class?
- Was the teacher able to modify the approach, pace, or level of work?
- Was there a recognition by the teacher when attention was lost by some or all of the class, and appropriate action taken?
- Was he/she able to stimulate the children?

- What comment have you to make about the teacher's vitality and imagination?
- Was the teacher clearly interested in the subject himself/herself and able to enthuse the children?
- How far did the quality of her/his speech aid or detract from the quality of the lesson?
- How did the teacher contribute to bring everyone into the lesson?

How well are resources used?
- Are the children given adequate resources for the task?
- Are the materials accessible and do they encourage independence?
- Has work been planned, taking into account the need to avoid all needing the same thing at the same time?
- Has provision been made for the safe use of resources?
- Is the teacher aware of the range of resources outside the school?
- Is IT being used appropriately?
- Is the classroom environment used as a resource?
- Are written materials such as worksheets user-friendly, well structured, concise, free from errors and where appropriate, differentiated?
- Do children know how to use the resources properly?

How well is the work organised?
- Is there a good layout of furniture to suit her/his approach to teaching?
- Have follow-up activities been planned?
- Are children given increasing responsibility for the way they work?
- Is the grouping appropriate and likely to lead to progress being made?
- Is there clear progression built into the lesson which provides opportunities for a variety of outcomes?
- Do displays reflect work in progress; act as a stimulus for further work; and reflect children's achievements?
- Are general resources organised in such a way that they are accessible to children and allow children to be 'self-servicing'?
- Have routines been worked out which provide order to the room and day?

- Were the arrangements for the storage of children's work, resources, and other possessions adequate?
- Are the children responsible for aspects of the organisation and able to do these tasks effectively?

How good is the classroom discipline and relationships with pupils?
- Is there a calm, relaxed atmosphere in which learning can flourish?
- Is there an opportunity for pupils to cooperate and develop social skills?
- Does the teacher show an ability to manage and control pupils in a variety of situations?
- Are there obvious conflict resolution strategies for coping with individual problems?
- Is there a good match of task and ability?
- Is the pace appropriate?
- Are the pupils purposeful and on-task?
- Does the teacher show an awareness of differences between groups and individuals?
- Is the teacher approachable, understanding, sympathetic?
- Does the teacher demonstrate effective listening skills and does she respond to personal news and events?
- Does the teacher use her voice to give clear instructions and does she also use non-verbal communication?
- Is mutual respect between teachers and pupils seen and does this include good manners?
- Is there a framework of clear and sensible rules which the children observe and do pupils demonstrate an understanding of classroom rules?
- How does the teacher react to children who break the rules?
- Is there an ordered freedom about the class?
- Subject to the type of activity, are the children able to move about to get the things they need?
- Is the teacher able to get the attention of the whole class when he/she needs it?
- How aware is the classteacher of everything going on in the room?
- How does he/she exercise control over the lesson? over the children? over group activities? Was the control unobtrusive or overt?

- How well does the teacher choose the time and manner of his/her intervention in group activities?
- How much interest, understanding and involvement of the children was shown?
- Were the children enthusiastic about what they were being told, or invited to do?
- Were they keen to take part either on an individual or group basis?
- Did the teacher have to go over much of the work with some or all of the class because they did not comprehend what he/she was attempting to do?
- How relaxed is the teacher with the children at various points of the day?
- Is it evident that he/she respects and likes children? Is this reciprocated?
- How does he/she address children? How do they respond and address him/her?
- Does he/she relate to boys more than girls or vice versa; one group more than another; have favourites; avoid selecting children for special activities?
- Does he/she develop special relationships with a new child, those in distress and special need? Does he/she involve the children in this caring activity?

How good is the assessment and feedback to children?
- Is assessment part of the planning process?
- Do they relate to the lesson objectives?
- Did the teacher question the children regularly and skilfully to determine what had been learnt?
- How well did he/she use this feedback to recapitulate or try a different approach?
- Did he/she check understanding with the children as a class or on an individual basis?
- How did he/she make observations about successes and failures in his/her lessons?
- How well does he/she report on children's progress?
- Does he/she look at or assess, including marking, work during the period?
- What attention does he/she give to handwriting and general presentation of work?
- Are the children involved in self-evaluation of their work?
- Does the teacher use the full range of assessment techniques?

- Are recording methods thought through?
- How are the results of assessment used?
- How did he/she make observations about successes and failures in his/her lessons?
- Does he/she understand the different purposes of, and terminology associated with, different forms of assessment i.e. (formative, summative, diagnostic and evaluation).
- Are evaluations perceptive, detailed and clearly organised, giving a full perspective on pupil attainment, teaching ability?

Is the classroom and teaching environment attractive?
- To what extent could the room be considered an attractive place for the children to work in?
- What efforts had the teacher made to provide a stimulating and educationally useful environment?
- Were there particular areas of interest within the room?
- Had the children been involved in any way in creating these areas?
- Were they able to make use of the materials and exhibits there?
- Were the classroom displays related to what was going on in the room?
- To what extent was children's work used?
- How many children were represented in the display?
- How long has the display been in place?
- How carefully had the teacher mounted the children's work?
- Was the work referred to in any way?
- Had the room a neat and tidy appearance without 'tat' on windowsills, on top of cupboards, in corners etc?
- What efforts has the teacher made to keep unfinished art, craft, etc. tidy?
- How are the children of the class involved in keeping the room in a satisfactory condition?

How effective was the lesson in promoting learning?
- Does the lesson represent a careful selection of worthwhile experiences, activities and opportunities for each child?

- Can it be seen as part of the development in a sequence of learning?
- Does the choice of lesson material and the adopted approach illustrate an understanding of the needs and nature of children at that particular stage in their primary schooling?
- Were you able to judge the success of the lesson by the verbal responses of the children and the written or creative responses?
- Was the lesson suitable for this group of children?
- Was the success universal or were there children who did not understand or gain a great deal and others who were bored and were not 'stretched'?
- Did the children appear to work hard?
- Did the lesson link with items previously taught and learnt?
- Did the children have an opportunity to show personal initiative in the set tasks?

There now follows a subject specific checklist for each curriculum subject and for observation of early years classrooms.

Self inspection activities for Primary Subject Leaders — ENGLISH

What you need to do	check ✗ ✔	comment

Go into lessons and look for evidence of pupils' acquisition, practice and application of key writing skills such as note-taking, revision and re-drafting of work and their achievements and difficulties in reading. Do children speak clearly, and confidently, do they compare, evaluate? Hypothesise, join in open-ended discussion? Do children reflect upon what each other says? Can they identify main points in what they have read, can they find and re-work information, use a dictionary, write neatly and legibly, vary their style to suit the purpose?

Talk with a variety of children from selected classes. Listen to them read a variety of texts and discuss the story. Can they predict what might happen next? Use the opportunity to discuss their reading habits such as why they choose some books in preference to others; their attitudes towards reading; how much reading they do at home, in school; if they belong to a local library etc.

Look at children's written work from a variety of classes. Can you see a range of different styles; are audiences important; how well do children use the English language? Have you seen informal and formal writing; word processed work and later re-edited work; can you see plays; reported speech; diaries, work for display? What progress is being made by children with special educational needs? How is work marked? Do comments look like they will be useful to children to know what they need to do to progress?

Look at teacher's planning and consider if it shows evidence of supporting continued progress in reading for children of different abilities. How are children of different attainment catered for? Are parents involved in supporting children's reading?

Read: Walters* and Martin (1998a)
          Coordinating English at Key Stage 1
or   Walters* and Martin (1998b)
          Coordinating English at Key Stage 2
also   Ray* (1995a) and Birch (1995) for KS1
          Ray* (1995b) and Roberts (1995) for KS2
*Mick Waters is an OFSTED Registered Inspector
*Rita Ray is an OFSTED team inspector

Self inspection activities for Primary Subject Leaders — MATHEMATICS

What you need to do	check ✗ ✔	comment

Go into lessons and work with small groups and ask questions. Ask how tasks were carried out; ask similar questions in a range of contexts. See what pupils know by heart and what they can figure out. How quick are pupils at mental calculation; what strategies do they use? How are children grouped? Is this appropriate? How much time do teachers spend teaching and how much just responding to problems? What progress is being made by children with IEPs?

Talk with a variety of children from selected classes to see how quickly they can recall number bonds and tables facts; how well they know mathematical terms such as cuboid and angles. Do children know how to break problems into constituent parts such as when creating LOGO procedures? Can they use calculators and number apparatus well? Can they recognise if answers are reasonable?

Look at children's maths work in books and workbooks. Can you see a range of different work in each class? How frequently do children do written mathematics work? Is the work completed? What evidence is there of each attainment target? What is the balance between them? Are you satisfied with the volume of work? How is work marked? Do comments look like they will be useful to children to know what they need to do to progress? Do children do 'corrections'/ Is this the same for all classes or is this just up to the teacher? Do pupils self-assess?

Examine teacher's planning, is it in line with the school scheme? Does it show work planned beyond the basic commercial text book; is work stimulating or dull; is there sufficient consolidation; is it challenging; do children have sufficient opportunities for practical mathematics? How does numeracy feature on the teaching of other subjects?

Read: Brown* (1998) *Coordinating mathematics across the primary school* in this series
also Stewart and Hocking (1995) and Harrison* (1995a) and NNP (1998) *National Numeracy Project Lessons*
*Tony Brown is an OFSTED inspector
*Mike Harrison is an OFSTED Rgl

Self inspection activities for Primary Subject Leaders — SCIENCE

What you need to do	check ✗ ✔	comment

Go into lessons and observe small groups at work and ask questions. How are children grouped? Is this appropriate? Ask children how tasks being undertaken were set up: Find out how much previous experience pupils have had at investigating and sorting materials; making circuits etc. See what science pupils know and what they can work out by using previous knowledge. How good are pupils at observing, sharing ideas. Do pupils seek to improve their experiments? Is due attention paid to health and safety issues?

Talk with a variety of children to assess how much they understand about sound, electricity, forces etc. Do children know why they carry out experiments? Can they draw conclusions from what they have found?. Do children find surprises? Do children know how to use books and other resources to further their investigations? What progress is being made by children with IEPs? What can pupils tell you about natural phenomena such as sunrise, the growth and behaviour of plants and animals, the weather? What attitude do children show to their work in science? Are they curious, do they try to explain what they see? Do they show respect and care for the environment?

Look at children's written work from a variety of classes. Can you see a range of work in each class covering all attainment targets? What is the balance between them? How frequently do children record their science work? Is the work completed? Are different methods of recording results employed? What evidence is there of coverage of each attainment target? How is the work marked? Is sufficient attention given to scientific content or is marking only for grammar and spellings? Do comments look like they will be useful to children to know what they need to do to progress in science? Are children corrected if their conclusions are inaccurate? Is this the same for all classes or is this just up to the teacher? Is scientific vocabulary being developed?

Look at teacher's planning and consider if it shows work planned to support, develop and build on knowledge and understanding, as well as to develop scientific skills. Is the work stimulating or dull; is there sufficient consolidation; is it challenging; do children have sufficient opportunities to develop their own experiments or do they all follow the teacher's pattern? How does the development of numeracy, literacy and IT feature in the teaching of science?

Read: Newton and Newton (1998)
         Coordinating science across the primary school
also   Bowe (1995) and Cross* and Byrne* (1995)
*Dave Byrne is an OFSTED Rgl
*Alan Cross is an OFSTED subject inspector.

Self inspection for Subject Leaders — INFORMATION AND COMMUNICATIONS TECHNOLOGY

What you need to do	check ✗ ✔	comment

Carry out a series of unannounced snapshot visits to classrooms in order to determine the level of use of computers in the classroom (an example survey form is reproduced at the end of this chapter p. 155) Consider what fraction of their maximum capacity is being used; what programs are largely being used on a day to day basis; does this fit with the whole school plan? Are you happy with this? How are children grouped around the computer? Is this appropriate? How much time do teachers spend teaching and intervening and how much just responding to problems?

Go into classrooms and observe children at work on the computer and using other ICT apparatus and ask them questions. Ask how tasks were set and find out if the work relates to a range of contexts. See what pupils know how to do. Can they load their own applications? Can they save files to disc and then later edit the work? Can pupils use the mouse, use on screen menus, can they load printer drivers and make hard copies of their work? Can they use a Roamer, sensing apparatus can they investigate a CD-ROM encyclopaedia well? Do children use research engines on the Internet, Does this relate to other investigations in the class? What progress is being made by children with IEPs?

Talk with a variety of children from selected classes to see how much time they have spent using ICT apparatus. Are you satisfied with this? What skills do they bring from home? Have they been able to use these in school? Do children remember working with LOGO; can they break problems into constituent parts when creating LOGO procedures? Can they describe some of the uses of computers and other ICT applications in work and society?

Look at work. Can you see a range of computer work in each class? Are there displays of children's work on the computer? What feedback do children get?

Look at teacher's planning, is it in line with the school scheme? Does it show ICT work planned to fit in with class topics? Is work stimulating or routine; is there sufficient consolidation; what are teachers' attitudes; are they committed?

Read: Harrison* (1998)
          Coordinating ICT across the primary school
also   Birch* (1995) KS1 and Harrison* (1995b) KS2
*Mike Harrison is an OFSTED RgI
*Tony Birch is an OFSTED team inspector

Self inspection activities for Primary Subject Leaders — DESIGN and TECHNOLOGY

What you need to do	check ✗ ✔	comment

Go into lessons and work with small groups of children designing and making. Ask how the tasks were started; find out if children have used similar skills in a range of contexts. Observe the way children work and look at pupils' drawings, their writing and the products they make. See what pupils know about developing designs and conveying their ideas to others. What knowledge do children have about the properties of the materials they are using, the skills they will need to make the artefacts and the likelihood of success? What strategies do they use to test out ideas? Do pupils evaluate their products and can they suggest improvements? How are children grouped? Is this appropriate? How much time do teachers spend teaching skills and facts and how much just responding to pupils with problems? What provision is made for pupils with special educational needs?

Talk with a variety of children to assess if they can modify designs; know why they are making the intended product; what tools they will need to use; what difficulties they are finding and the strategies they have to solve these problems.

Look at samples of children's work which may be in books, as completed products or recorded in photographs and on video. Can you see a range of different work in each class? Is the work completed? What evidence is there of both designing and making? What is the balance between specific skills teaching and design and make projects?

Examine teacher's planning to determine whether it is in line with the school scheme. How frequently do children appear to do work in D&T? Does it show work planned which is challenging; is there sufficient consolidation; do children have sufficient opportunities to evaluate and amend their designs and their products? How does the development of numeracy and literacy feature in the teaching of D&T? What feedback do pupils get?

Read: Cross (1998) *Coordinating design and technology across the primary school*
also   Boekestein (1995) KS1 and Cross*
              (1995) KS2
*Alan Cross is an OFSTED team inspector

Self inspection activities for Primary Subject Leaders — HISTORY

What you need to do   check ✗ ✔   comment

Go into lessons, observe children in history lessons. Are learning
objectives appropriate, are the activities likely to achieve them? Is use
being made of appropriate resources? How are children responding to
the teaching? Do pupils reflect upon what they have been taught; do they
refer to previous learning? Ask children about the work they are doing —
how were the tasks introduced; find out if children have used similar skills
in a range of contexts. What progress is being made by children with
IEPs? Observe the way children work together. Do they use appropriate
vocabulary — and look at pupils' drawings, their writing and other output.
Do they report critically on the evidence with which they are presented?.
See what pupils know by asking 'How were things different then — how
do we know that?'. What knowledge do children have about the truth of
the evidence they are using? What skills do they have to make sense of
the facts they are told. What strategies do they use to test out ideas? Do
pupils evaluate evidence and can they suggest alternative explanations?

How are children grouped in the classroom? Is this appropriate? How
much time do teachers spend teaching skills and facts and how much
responding to pupils with problems? How is feedback given? Is work
marked for historical facts or interpretations or merely for grammar
and spelling?

Talk with a variety of children to see if they can pursue a
historical enquiry; if they know why they are studying a certain topic;
what resources they will need to use; what difficulties they are finding
and the strategies they have to solve these problems.

Look at children's work in books and folders. Is there evidence of
visits to museums ad historical sites? What use is made of such first-hand
experiences? Can you see a range of different work in each class? Is the
work completed? What is the balance between giving information, such
as in stories and narrative, and encouraging enquiry?

Examine teachers' planning. Does it incorporate specific objectives or
is it merely a backdrop to writing for a topic? How frequently do children
appear to do work in history? Is it in line with the school scheme? Does
it show in work planned which is challenging; introduces children to an
expanding knowledge base; allows them to develop an understanding of
the sequence of historical periods and gives them access to a good range
of source materials? How much does the development of numeracy and
literacy feature in the plans for teaching history? What assessment is
common?

Read: Davies and Redmond (1998)
               Coordinating history across the primary school
also   Davies (1995a) KS1 and Davies (1995b) KS2
and *Beat the Inspector Laar** (1998) *Bill Laar is an OFSTED Rgl

© Falmer Press

Self inspection activities for Primary Subject Leaders — GEOGRAPHY

What you need to do   check ✗ ✔   comment

Go into geography lessons, observe the teaching and work with small groups of children. Ask how the activities were started; find out if children have used similar generic skills in a range of contexts. Observe the way children work and look at pupils' drawings, their writing and see what they do about conveying their ideas to others. What knowledge do children have about the aspect they are studying? Can the pupils use a map; can they recognise patterns and processes, do they respect causality? Do children use appropriate geographical terminology? What progress is being made by children with IEPs?

How are children grouped in the lesson? Is this appropriate? How much time do teachers spend teaching skills and facts and how much just responding to pupils with problems? Is work marked to aid learning of geography or for grammar and spellings only. Are you happy about this?

Talk with a variety of children to see if they can explain similarities and differences between places; use geographical skills in their instigation of themes; know why they are studying a topic; what skills they will need to find out more; what difficulties they are finding and strategies they have to solve such problems.

Look at samples of children's work which may be in books or folders. Can you see a range of different work in each class? Is the work usually completed? What evidence is there of knowledge and understanding of place and a range of geographical themes? What is the balance between specific skills teaching and providing a backdrop for class projects? What evidence exists of the use of photographs, videos and field visits?

Look at teachers' planning. How frequently do children appear to do geography work? Is teacher's planning in line with the school scheme? Does it show challenging and interesting work planned; is there sufficient consolidation; do children have sufficient opportunities to evaluate and amend their designs and their products? How does the development of numeracy and literacy feature in the teaching of geography? What is the quality of feedback to pupils?

Read: Halocha (1998)
         Coordinating geography across the primary school
also   Rodger* (1995) KS1 and Boyle (1995) KS2
*Rosemary Rodger is an OFSTED Rgl

Self inspection activities for Primary Subject Leaders — ART

What you need to do	check ✗ ✔	comment

Go into lessons where art, craft and design is the focus and work with small groups of children involved in investigating and/or making art. Can pupils select from and use a range of materials and stimulus; are they able to evaluate and modify their work; are they acquiring and consolidating new skills and techniques? Are they able to use tools safely? Ask how the activities were introduced; find out if children have used similar skills in other contexts. Observe the way children work and look at pupils' drawings, their paintings and the other products they make. How do children respond to visual stimuli? Do pupils evaluate their products and can they suggest improvements?

How are children grouped? Is this appropriate? How much time do teachers spend teaching skills and how much just responding to pupils with problems? How are pupils with special educational needs provided for?

Talk with a variety of children to see if they can explain why they have chosen the paint, pastel, collage etc; do they know why they are making the intended art product; what tools they will need to use; what difficulties they are finding and the strategies they have to solve these problems? What knowledge do children have about the properties of the materials they are using, the skills they will need to finish the work? What do pupils think of their work? Do pupils express themselves using the appropriate terminology?

Look at children's work which may be in sketchbooks, portfolios or on display. What do you think of the quality and finish to the work? Can you see a range of different work in each class? Is there evidence of the use of a variety of media? Is the work completed? What evidence is there of both investigating and making? What is the balance between specific skills teaching and work to illustrate other subjects?

Look at teachers' plans. Do teachers value children's art work? Is it well displayed? Do teachers have an understanding of art; have they created visually pleasing environments? Is teacher's planning for art in line with the school scheme? How frequently do children appear to do this work? Does planning show work which is challenging; is there sufficient consolidation; do children have sufficient opportunities to evaluate and amend or repeat their work? What feedback do pupils get? If adult helpers are used are they properly briefed?

Read: Piotrowski, Clements and Roberts (1998)
        Coordinating art across the primary school
also   Ray* (1995c) KS1 and Piotrowski (1995) KS2
*Rita Ray is an OFSTED team inspector

Self inspection activities for Primary Subject Leaders — MUSIC

What you need to do   check ✗ ✔   comment

Go into a number of classrooms and focus on pupil's
performing and composing; and listening and appraising in
the context of the music lesson, which is likely to be the
whole music curriculum for the majority of the pupils.
Ask how the activities were designed and how they relate
to skills used in a range of contexts. Observe the way
children work when performing and composing and assess
how much musical knowledge they are gaining in the
lesson. How are they conveying their ideas to others?
Do pupils evaluate their performances and can they
suggest improvements?

How are children grouped? How are pupils with special
educational needs provided for? Is good use made of
time and resources? How much time do teachers spend
teaching skills and how much responding to pupils with
problems? Are challenges set and what strategies do
children use to test out ideas? Do teachers encourage
high quality performances and compositions; do they help
pupils to develop an appropriate music vocabulary?

Talk with a variety of children to assess their
knowledge and understanding of music; what instruments
they know about and what will they need to use to achieve
their purposes. Do children listen to music? How do they
express their appreciation?

Look at children's work which may be recorded on
tape and on video. Is there a range of different work in
each class? What evidence is there of both performing and
composing?

Look at teachers' planning. Is teacher's planning in
line with the school scheme? How frequently do children
appear to do work in music? Does it show work planned
which is challenging; is there sufficient consolidation; do
children have sufficient opportunities to evaluate and
practise their performances? What feedback to pupils get?

Read: Hennessy (1998)
           Coordinating music across the primary school
also   Walker (1995) KS1 and Walker (1995) KS2

Self inspection activities for Primary Subject Leaders — PHYSICAL EDUCATION

What you need to do	check ✗ ✔	comment

Go into PE lessons and observe groups of children planning performing and evaluating activities. Are learning objectives clear? Consider how the tasks are introduced; is there sufficient opportunity for children develop similar skills they have learned in other contexts? Observe the way children plan and watch their performances. See how sophisticated the pupils' movements have become as they move up through the school. What are pupils able to do in the various strands which comprise the PE curriculum? Can pupils work in pairs to develop sequences of movements? How smooth are the transitions from one movement to another? Do children test out ideas? Do pupils evaluate their work and can they suggest improvements?

How well do children work in groups? How much of teachers' time is spent teaching skills and how much responding to pupils with problems? Is time used well? How quickly do children change and get ready for the activities? Is there appropriate attention to warm-up and warm-down activities? Does the teacher choose appropriate examples of good practice to demonstrate to the rest of the class? How are pupils with special educational needs provided for?

Talk with a variety of children to provide evidence of their knowledge and understanding; know why they are making the movements; what might the group do differently; what do they feel about teamwork; vigorous activity; various games and sports? Can pupils observe the movements of others in dance or gymnastics; can they report what they see? Do they appreciate the need for rules in a game or the effects of exercise on the body?

Look at any videos of children doing PE, examine records of achievements. Can you see a range of different work in each class? What evidence is there of both planning and performing? What is the balance between specific skills teaching and playing games?

Look at teachers' planning. Is it in line with the school scheme? How frequently do children appear to do PE? What aspect of the subject appears least often? Are there signs of increasing complexity or more difficult contexts to ensure progression? Is the work planned challenging; is there sufficient consolidation; do children have sufficient opportunities to evaluate and improve their skills? What feedback do pupils get? Are teachers giving safety a high priority?

Read: Raymond (1998) *Coordinating physical education across the primary school*
also   Chedzoy (1995) KS1 and Sanderson (1995) KS2

Self inspection activities for Primary Subject Leaders — RELIGIOUS EDUCATION

What you need to do	check ✗ ✔	comment

Go into lessons and work with small groups of children engaged in religious studies. Find out if children have used similar skills of enquiry in a range of contexts. Observe the way children work and look at pupils' drawings and their writing. Are they able to able to appreciate the religious traditions they have been taught? See what pupils know about religious issues and the application of religious traditions to everyday life. What understanding do they have of religious concepts and symbolism? How are children grouped in the lesson? Is this appropriate? How much time do teachers spend teaching ideas and facts and how much responding to pupils with problems? What is the quality of feedback to pupils?

What artefacts, pictures and other resources exist for the teaching of this subject?

Talk with a variety of children to see if correct terminology is being used when describing say, religious traditions in the area. Can children tell you about various religious artefacts, buildings, ceremonies? Do they know how to find out information to extend their enquiries?

Look at samples of children's work which may be in books, folders or part of a topic. Can you see a range of different work in each class? Is the work completed? What evidence is there of all aspects of the agreed syllabus? What is the balance between religious education teaching and using religious symbolism as a backdrop to a topic?

Examine teachers' planning to see if it is in line with the school scheme. How frequently do children appear to do work in RE? Does it show work planned which is challenging; is there sufficient opportunity for pupils to re-visit aspects of RE, are they encouraged to follow up their work in school, at home; do children have sufficient opportunities to discuss the beliefs of others? How does the use and development of literacy feature in the teaching of RE? What provision is made for pupils with IEPs to gain full access to the RE curriculum?

Read: Bastide (1998) *Coordinating religious education across the primary school*

also   Mattock and Preston (1995) and Mattock (1995)

Self inspection activities for Primary Subject Leaders — EARLY YEARS

What you need to do	check **X ✔**	comment

Go into lessons, observe the teaching and work with small groups of children. Ask about the activities; find out if children have used similar generic skills in a range of contexts. Observe whether children listen attentively and talk about their experiences. Do they listen and respond to stories, songs, nursery rhymes. Look at pupils' drawings, their emergent writing and see what they do about conveying their ideas to others. What knowledge do children have about the world around them? Can the pupils use a pencil, crayon, brush? Can they recognise patterns and name colours? Do children use appropriate words to talk about the things in the classroom? What progress is being made by children in literacy and numeracy?

How are children grouped in the lesson? Is this appropriate? How much time do teachers and nursery staff spend teaching skills and facts and how much just responding to pupils with problems? Are children praised and encouraged in their work. Do children seem enthusiastic?

Talk with a variety of children to see if they can tell you about numbers, shapes, pattern; do they have developing physical skills; know why they are doing the work set; what skills they will need to find out more; what difficulties they are finding and determine the strategies they have to solve such problems.

Look at samples of children's work which may be in books or folders. Can you see a range of different work? Is the work usually completed? What evidence is there of progression? What is the balance between specific skills teaching and providing a backdrop for projects? What evidence exists of the use of materials, games, artefacts in the teaching?

Look at teachers' planning. How frequently do children appear to do different types of work? Is teacher's planning in line with the school scheme? Does it show challenging and interesting work planned; is there sufficient consolidation;? How does the development of numeracy and literacy feature in the teaching. What is the quality of feedback to parents?

2 minute snapshot survey into the use of computers in school

This form relates to ONE computer — prepare one for each computer in your school

Time and date of survey: Tuesday 11:15am / Thursday 1:45pm etc.

This computer is a BBC/BBC 128/Ach 3020/A4000/A5000/A7000 other ....
PC type ....
Research machine (RM) type ....
Macintosh type ....
Other type ....

It is located in   classroom Y/N   corridor Y/N
                   spare classroom Y/N   library   Y/N other ....

At the time above the computer was
         switched off   Y/N
         switched on but no program showing   Y/N
         program showing but not being used   Y/N
         computer being used by .. Girls and. .. Boys in Year ....
         Other ....   Y/N

The reason it was not being used was
         machine broken   Y/N
         no suitable program available   Y/N
         other whole-class activity planned   Y/N
         Other ....   Y/N

The machine was being used:
         by individual or group using program/application   Y/N
         to demonstrate to the whole class   Y/N
         by a series of pupils to add data part of investigation   Y/N
         to connect to the Internet   Y/N
         to communicate by e-mail   Y/N
         for video conferencing   Y/N
         Other ....   Y/N

The program or application being used at the time was:
         a word processor (name ....)   Y/N
         a database (name ....)   Y/N
         an art package (name ....)   Y/N
         a logo type package (name ....)   Y/N
         a music programme (name ....)   Y/N
         a simulation (name ....)   Y/N
         an adventure program (name ....)   Y/N
         for research (CD-ROM investigation/ encyclopaedia) (name ....)   Y/N
         specific IT skills training (name ....)   Y/N

Any other observation on the use of this particular computer at the time of the survey

In addition to the forms of monitoring and evaluation we have now discussed and which will be carried out by you personally, you may at some stage wish to consider the support which might be offered by some kind of external monitoring. Local education authority inspection and advisory services and advisory teachers, staff of local higher education institutions (HEIs) and other consultants can all offer a valuable outside view, perhaps identifying issues which are not obvious to you. Where such external help is used it is important to establish the focus for their work, the criteria they will be using and what you can expect as feedback.

You will wish to keep your school's SMT and governing body informed of the outcomes of your monitoring activities. This will be particularly true where there appears to be a need for action which is outside the scope of your normal responsibilities.

As you will see, your monitoring and evaluation activities will have led to the amassing of a considerable amount of information and should therefore have identified key elements in the action plan which forms the focus of the next chapter.

Action planning and setting targets

Trying to set a rigid and formulaic school development plan, given the rate of change in the educational world,

> seems merely to be about tailoring another article of the emperor's clothing. Strategic intent, however, is not only possible but an imperative. The summit of the mountain is clearly photographed. Everyone knows what it looks like and shares the passion to get there. The school is going to get to that summit at some time in the next five years. At present many of the possible routes are covered in cloud, there are rumours of avalanches, and it is known that there is a tribe of wild bears roaming about . . . the path is not at all clear . . . The summit will remain. The passion and the clarity of the vision inform every act, every piece of paper, every decision.
>
> Bowring-Carr and West-Burnham (1997)

Your monitoring and evaluation activities will inevitably reveal in a definitive way the areas of your subject or area that you wish to develop and improve. It will probably be the case also that the OFSTED inspection itself will have identified strengths and weaknesses in your subject or area of responsibility. You will want to analyse the inspection report in this regard as well as review any information you have received in feedback from the inspectors. In the event that your subject or area has been identified in the key issues for action in the report, there will be significant implications for your future development of the subject and how you go about it. Whatever the case, this chapter is about what targets for improvement you might set and the ways in which you can plan the actions to achieve those targets. But do not forget that setting unrealistic goals which cannot be achieved will not help anyone — least of all you!

Action planning

We begin by looking at some general principles of action planning. It is likely that any action plan you are involved in formulating and monitoring in its implementation will be part of a wider school development plan. The nature and contents of such a whole school plan should be the result of a systematic audit process. Effective schools have always followed such a process but in any case now, all schools will be involved in development planning as they respond to their inspection reports with the statutorily required post-OFSTED action plan. Where your particular plan fits in with the whole school plan will be influenced by the school's priorities and any priorities identified in your inspection report. But your 'individual' plan will be contributing to the successful achievement of the whole plan. It should define individual and collective responsibilities; time schedules and target dates; the nature and availability of support, including staff development and in-service training; the estimated costs and resources required to achieve the plan's targets.

Your action plan should enable everyone involved to know:
■ what is to be done;
■ why it is to be done;
■ who is to do it;
■ what support and\or training is needed;
■ by when it is to be done;
■ how much it will cost;
■ what help is available;
■ the means whereby progress through the plans will be monitored;
■ the criteria by which successful achievement of the plan will be judged.

The process of action planning

The following are the stages through which you will need to go in drawing up, implementing, monitoring and reviewing and evaluating your action plan.

1 Establishing priority needs, which as indicated will emerge to some extent from the whole school audit of need, or as a result of what OFSTED have to say about your school. However, within your subject or area the audit will identify another set of priorities which will need to be addressed. For example, as mathematics coordinator you may identify one of the attainment targets as being badly covered, say data handling, and your plan will prioritise this area. Your early years curriculum may be weak in developing children's knowledge and understanding of the world, and action needed to improve this will be the focus of your action planning responsibility as early years coordinator.

2 As a result of the audit process (which will be based largely on the monitoring and evaluation processes identified in the previous chapter) you should be able to state clearly the current situation. Or indeed, as indicated, your inspection report may give an accurate picture of where you are up to.

3 You should then be able to describe the desired outcomes of your plan: articulating clear success criteria. We go on to say more about this in a moment, but it is critical to the success of the plan that everyone is clear at the outset about what is to be achieved. It is about smart target-setting.

4 Detail the steps which now need to be taken to achieve the desired outcome. This is the action plan itself, involving the issues of personnel, time, cost and resources, support and training already referred to.

5 Judge the extent to which your success criteria have been achieved, the evaluation stage, which will again depend heavily on your monitoring routines.

6 Validate the achievement of the plan, which will be easier to do in terms of the evidence of achievement if the success criteria were specific and measurable in the first place.

7   Report to whoever needs to know the progress in your plan,
    what has or has not been achieved so that it can be fed back
    into the next audit and the planning and improvement
    cycle can begin again, hopefully at a higher level of
    operation.

Success criteria

A good action plan will be

Smart
Measurable
Attainable
Relevant
Time-constrained

Success criteria attempt to define the situation which will exist
when the targets of the action plan have been attained. It is
important that success criteria are considered very early in the
action planning process, ideally following the review stage. In
this way, success criteria can define and help to drive the plan
towards the targets. Evidence in support of the success criteria
should be monitored and noted throughout the period of the
action plan. This is perhaps particularly important for criteria
where it is more difficult to make judgments about success at a
single point in time, for example indications of changes in
children's' attitudes towards reading or their enjoyment of
mathematics. Ultimately, whatever success criteria are used to
indicate a plan's success, the achievement of targets must be
judged on the extent to which they have enhanced the quality
of educational provision and learning, in its broadest sense, in
the school.

Success criteria should:
■   refer to future performance;
■   relate to a planned target designed to improve the quality of
    educational provision and the learning which it promotes;
■   be chosen by the people who draw up the plans and set the
    targets;
■   influence the way the targets are designed;

- be verifiable to others as evidence of success, which again has implications for the specificity and measurability of the criteria set.

Success criteria are valuable in a broader sense in that they support schools in their overall development and improvement. They identify and promote the school's desired goals and suggest the standards appropriate to such goals. They clearly guide the actions needed to achieve the agreed goals. This is about putting flesh on the bones of the often fairly general overall aims and objectives that schools write for themselves. Statements such as *We strive to ensure that each child reaches his or her full potential, achieving the highest possible standards* are empty rhetoric in the absence of a clear and measurable definition of what it means in practice. Thus success criteria can help to distinguish between aspiration, process and outcome, indicate the evidence needed to judge success and contribute to the overall evaluation of the school's progress in achieving its stated developmental aims. They are a good way of helping and involving people in school, as well as those carrying out an outside review, such as inspectors, in judging its success. And the achievement of success is an excellent basis for the next stage of planning!

Target setting

The setting of specific and measurable targets which focus primarily on pupils' attainment is increasingly seen as the most effective basis for establishing effective success criteria for your action plans. OFSTED analyses of school development planning and post-inspection action plans indicated that few schools were setting specific targets for the improvement of achievement or had developed criteria or indicators against which to monitor and evaluate the effectiveness of any proposed action in terms of raised standards. Inspection has shown that internal review and target setting are often the weakest parts of schools' planning cycles. Specific targets aimed at raising standards are seldom set.

❝ *Action plans are primarily concerned with raising achievement. The best plans are drawn up consultatively by governors, the headteacher and staff and incorporate:*

- *specific targets for raising standards or improving quality of provision;*
- *practical strategies and programmes of development focused on these goals; and*
- *arrangements for monitoring and evaluating the progress and impact of measures taken.*

OFSTED (1995b) *Planning Improvement:*
Schools' Post-inspection Action plans. (p. 3)

As a coordinator you need to be familiar with this movement towards target setting focused on raising achievement, particularly if you coordinate a subject in which there is statutory testing and assessment. Inspectors will be using analyses of assessment results data when looking at school improvement in the re-inspection process. You too can be using assessment data in your review, action planning and evaluation processes and we shall be looking at ways in which you can do this.

The main materials with which you should make yourself familiar are the DfEE\OFSTED (1996) booklet *Setting Targets to Raise Standards: A Survey of Good Practice*, which states:

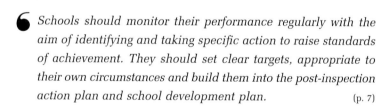 *Schools should monitor their performance regularly with the aim of identifying and taking specific action to raise standards of achievement. They should set clear targets, appropriate to their own circumstances and build them into the post-inspection action plan and school development plan.* (p. 7)

and *From Targets into Action: Guidance to Support Effective Target-setting in Schools* (DfEE, 1997) which indicates that the setting of school targets for the core subjects of English, mathematics and science will be compulsory.

School improvement

The concentration on target setting defined in this way is part of a wider national drive for school improvement which is articulated in current legislation. In order that you can be aware of and understand your coordination role and responsibilities within the context of school improvement, a context within which the inspectors who re-inspect your school will also be working, we identify its key principles.

School improvement is defined largely in terms of outcomes as higher standards of attainment, with particular emphasis on literacy and numeracy. Nevertheless, improvement in these areas has to be within a continuing statutory requirement for children to be given access to a broad and balanced curriculum. We have already noted the importance of all coordinators being aware of the ways in which these core skills are both developed and used within their own subjects. And there is no suggestion that the methods by which children are taught has no effect on these standards. All coordinators need to be aware of the content and methodology of the literacy and numeracy hours and how they might relate to their own subjects. The main strategic vehicle for school improvement is seen as development planning. The setting of specific, measurable targets for improving learning outcomes is seen as the key element within the plan.

There are two other important principles within school improvement. One is that improvement measured against baseline levels will indicate the extent to which a school has 'added value' to its pupils' learning and that the amount of value added is the fairest way of assessing a school's performance and comparing it with that of other schools. The influence of a range of factors on what a school can be reasonably expected to achieve by way of standards is recognised. They include social disadvantage; the proportion of pupils with special educational needs; the gender balance within cohorts of pupils; pupil mobility; the proportion of pupils for whom English is an additional language. For comparative purposes, therefore, the notion of benchmarking has been introduced.

Benchmarking is the process of measuring standards of actual performance against those achieved by others with broadly similar characteristics, setting targets for improvement and prioritising the actions necessary to reach the targets. Amongst a group of schools sharing similar characteristics, the benchmark represents the standard of performance achieved by the best members of the group and what should be achievable by all. It thus gives contextual information against which to set realistic targets for improvement. Generalised comparisons, with no contextualisation, mask the widely differing results achieved by similar intakes of pupils and the fact that some schools appear far more successful than others in helping pupils to achieve their full potential. Benchmarking, it is suggested, leads to schools asking questions such as:

- Why is it that some schools like ours can achieve results which appear so much better?
- What is it that these schools are doing that we can learn from?
- What progress can we make to achieve similar results?
- How should we plan that progress and over what period of time?

The five stage cycle for school improvement
1 How well are we doing?
2 How do we compare with similar schools?
3 What more should we aim to achieve this year?
4 What must we do to make it happen?
5 Have we made a difference?

All of these questions refer to the progress pupils are making in their learning and the standards they achieve.

Using assessment information for school improvement

This section will be particularly relevant if you coordinate English, mathematics or science, as it is in these subjects that National Curriculum test and assessment data is available and where other tests, such as norm-referenced standardised tests are most likely to be produced. It will also apply to all school managers, anyone with across key stage responsibility and assessment coordinators.

There are six key questions which the analysis of assessment data might help us to answer. How is our school currently performing overall in my subject? Are some parts — classes, key stages — more effective than others? Are some parts of my subject, for example reading within English, better or worse than others? Are some groups of pupils doing better than others, for example between boys and girls, or different ethnic groups? How do achievements in the subject now compare with previous achievements? How does our school's performance in the subject compare with that of other schools?

In terms of specific purposes, you can look at your subject's test and assessment results to see if:

■ your expectations are appropriate for all pupils;
■ there is improvement in relation to your baseline, allowing analysis of how much value you have added to pupils' learning;
■ boys and girls and any other relevant groups are achieving similar results;
■ some classes/key stages are performing better than others;
■ there are variations in performance within and between subjects;
■ your pupils do as well as those in similar schools when taking account of benchmarking information;
■ you know what you do well;
■ there are any year on year trends;
■ you have clear on-going evidence of the progress pupils are making in learning your subject;
■ you don't have too many surprises!

As well as analysing the results themselves, you might also wish to consider the actual task and test scripts which pupils complete, as they can indicate gaps in knowledge and understanding both for individuals and for the whole school.

A process for setting targets from assessment data

If you want to set targets for improvement in your subject so that they can be incorporated into your action plan success criteria as measurable increases in the proportion of pupils achieving, say a National Curriculum level or other criteria specified, you can do so by a generalised estimate or by a more systematic evaluation of what is reasonably possible in terms of the pupils you have. We assume that you will wish to approach the task through a coherent analysis of the data and information that you already hold on individuals and groups of pupils in your subject. Ideally such data will be routinely held and information can readily be dropped down from it. Computer software can be developed to enable the data to be efficiently held and easily interrogated. The following four stages are suggested as a basis for the target setting process.

Stage 1

Analyse the 'broad' data available from national and local sources: National Curriculum assessment comparative information and benchmarking. Examples of the nature and form in which this data is likely to be presented to you are given in Figures 9.1 and 9.2 below. Figure 9.1 shows the results in the Key Stage 1 spelling test of all primary schools in the LEA, indicating also the LEA average. Your school is shown as say, school number 20. As you will see it is operating significantly below the LEA average both in the number of children achieving the National Expectation (Level 2) and the level above this. Looked at in these crude terms the information is probably not very helpful to you as you may have similar results in many other areas of the curriculum. A more useful comparison will be with the performance of schools with similar characteristics to your own — in other words the benchmarked data. Figure 9.2 indicates that your school's performance when compared with other schools in the LEA which share similar levels of free school meal entitlement is close to the average. Therefore there may be other areas of the curriculum which more urgently require the school's attention. If however your school was represented by school 72 the problem would be clearly identified as underachievement in spelling.

It is now possible to compare your own school's performance in all end of key stage assessments by using the National Benchmarked information produced annually by the DfEE/QCA (1998). Figure 9.3 shows the results for a school which has added its results to the nationally benchmarked picture. This information for all schools with similar characteristics is presented in terms of the average performance for schools in the upper, middle and lower

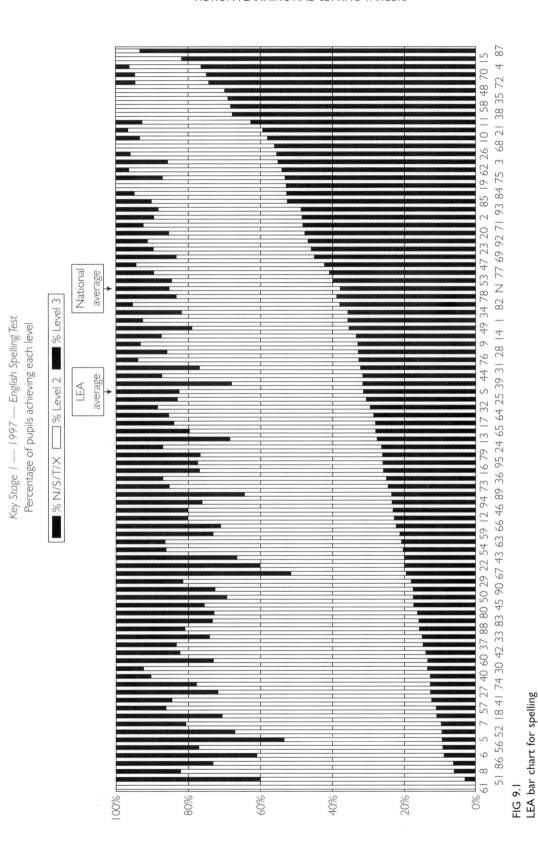

FIG 9.1
LEA bar chart for spelling

FIG 9.2
Comparison of performance
within an LEA

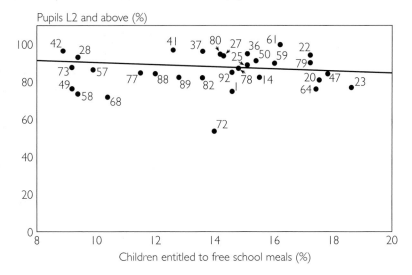

Key Stage 1 — 1997 — English Writing Test
Schools with 8.01–20.00% of pupils entitled to FSM

FIG 9.3
Benchmarked results

KS1 results, 1996; schools with up to 50% of EAL pupils and 20–35% taking FSM

Percentage of pupils achieving Level 2 and above.
Table 'exploded' to allow schools to plot their own results.

	95%		UQ		MED		LQ	
English								
TA	95		84	77	75		65	
Reading test	94		82		73	68	63	
Writing test	96		84	78	76		65	
Mathematics								
TA	98	92	88		80		70	
Test	98	93	88		80		70	
Science								
TA	100		91	85	82		76	

quartiles. This shows, therefore, the range of scores achieved by similar schools and allows you and your colleagues to compare like with like. For example Figure 9.3 showing the 1996 benchmarked results would indicate that it is doing well in mathematics but is underachieving in reading. This is obviously an area in which questions about the teaching and learning approaches will need to be raised.

Alongside this you will need to consider any other data you may have, for example from commercially produced standardised tests. This should make it possible to establish a clear view of the appropriate areas of your curriculum to be the subject of your targets for improvement, for example, if your scores in say, writing, are below national and local averages and you are at the lower end of your benchmarking cluster.

Stage 2

Further analysis may also help you to decide the type of target to be set. (See *From Targets to Action*, DfEE, 1997 p. 13) If you have a significant number of pupils not achieving the national expectation (Level 2 or Level 4 depending on the key stage) you may wish to set targets which are aimed primarily at lifting the attainment of more pupils to this **threshold**. If you have a favourably comparable number of pupils at the threshold levels, then you may wish to consider raising your **average** performance, by reducing numbers of pupils at low levels and\or increasing those achieving higher levels. Another type of target is what the DfEE booklet calls **reliability** targets. These set a floor of achievement below which you do not wish to drop. Types of target can be combined and the type of target you set will to a considerable extent determine the focus of your actions to achieve the target.

Stage 3

Once the area of focus and the type of target have been established, the next step is to decide the balance between challenge and realism in the actual, measurable target. (*From Targets to Action* identifies three 'zones' of targets: the historic, the comfort, the challenge and the unlikely. It is intended that

Activity 15

Using assessment information for school improvement in the primary school

Case Study: patterns of performance at Key Stages 1 and 2: Reading

Staff at this primary school were interested in looking at the profile of results for Key Stage 1 and Key Stage 2 in reading. Their recent OFSTED inspection report highlighted this as an area in which children were not achieving standards in line with national expectations, particularly at Key Stage 2. The graphs show performance in reading nationally and for the school in the tests at Key Stage 1, and for Key Stage 2 the national and school results for English, along with the school results for reading.

What issues might staff consider in their discussions and what kinds of strategies might be offered to begin to use and act upon the information they have from this data?

Activity 15a

Case Study: patterns of performance in En 2 (Reading) at KS1 and KS2

KS1 — national and school
%age of pupils

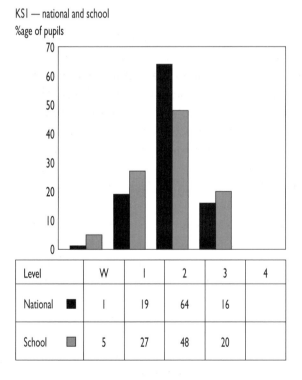

Level	W	1	2	3	4
National ■	1	19	64	16	
School ▨	5	27	48	20	

KS2 — national and school
%age of pupils

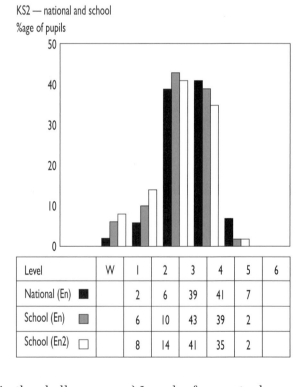

Level	W	1	2	3	4	5	6
National (En) ■		2	6	39	41	7	
School (En) ▨		6	10	43	39	2	
School (En2) ☐		8	14	41	35	2	

targets will be in the challenge zone.) In order for you to do this, there will need to be an analysis at the level of individual pupils within school year age cohorts. This implies the need for good knowledge about, and records of, pupils' performance in your subject and other factors you will need to take into consideration.

> ❝ Targets which do not improve on previous performance, could be justified where there is clear evidence that a year group is markedly less able than the others. In this case, a school may appear to have a target in the 'historic' zone, but is actually doing better than previously. The school will need good data about the relative strengths of different years, so that they can properly evaluate unexpected variations. (DfEE, 1997)

Targets will need to be based on your school's forecasts for the performance of its pupils. Such forecasts should be estimates of future performance based on evidence and realistically high expectations. The DfEE suggests that a good time to make such forecasts would be in the autumn term for performance in tests two years later. This provides a sensible time-scale for working with pupils on achieving or exceeding the forecasts.

The grid in Figure 9.4 indicates the type of information that might be taken account of in setting appropriate targets for individual pupils. The aggregation of these individual targets will constitute the school or class target for your subject. This can then be compared with previous performance and with how it stands in relation to meeting local and national targets and the success of your action planning process be measured.

Stage 4

Considering the stage represented on the grid in Figure 9.4 by the column 'Action to reach target'. This will be about the specific teaching and learning strategies to be employed and can thus be seen as the most important element of the target-setting cycle. It will constitute the major part of your action plan which will be rooted in the teaching and learning of your subject: its curriculum and how it is planned and resourced; the quality of teaching related to the learning objectives you have for the pupils; secure arrangements for managing pupils' behaviour; for assessing their progress; for working with their homes; for professional development in the subject and for all of the monitoring and evaluating of the quality of education provided in your subject throughout the school and the

NAME	AGE YEARS MONTHS	TIME IN THIS SCHOOL (Date of Entry)	FSM ✓	STAGE ON SEN REG.	EAL ✓	NURSERY/ PRE-SCHOOL ✓	BASELINE SCORE PRE KS1	KS 1 LEVEL TEST	TEACHER ASSESSMENT Y3 ATTAINMENT TARGET			
									1	2	3	4

FIG 9.4
Target setting — mathematics

TEACHER ASSESSMENT Y4 ATTAINMENT TARGET				TEACHER ASSESSMENT Y5 ATTAINMENT TARGET				OTHER TEST SCORES (NFER)	Y4 SAT (OPTIONAL)	CURRENT TA C = CIRCUMSTANCE	ACTION TO REACH TARGET	TARGET LEVEL
1	2	3	4	1	2	3	4					

© Falmer Press

FIG 9.4
cont.

standards of achievement it leads to: all of the issues, in short, dealt with in this handbook.

Actions may be seen as occurring at three levels: those relating to whole-school approaches e.g. improving the teaching of writing; introducing data-handling more consistently into the mathematics curriculum; those relating to specific groups of pupils e.g. the more able who seem capable of higher attainment in your subject, the group of pupils operating just below age related levels; those relating to individual pupils, of the kind already common in individual education plans of pupils with special educational needs.

The action planned may well include cooperation with schools of a similar kind which appear to be operating more effectively in the area targeted. For example, one school compared its end of Key Stage 1 spelling test results with another which had virtually the same FSM indicator. Whereas it had 54 per cent of children achieving Level 2, the similar school had over 90 per cent. Staff visits to the more successful school proved extremely useful in enabling teachers to see and consider alternative teaching approaches, some of which were later adopted by the school with lower results and seem likely to lead to higher standards.

Action plans — examples

The format in which action plans are presented are many and varied and the most important aspect — what you intend and how you achieve it — is the key! However, many subject coordinators will be helped by analysing the action plans presented here.

Example 1 — Review

Suggestion

Activity 16
Critically analyse the action plan presented by a design and technology coordinator as a result of her review. What essential features are missing?

The coordinator indicated that the teaching of design and technology throughout the school was lacking clear planning for continuity and progression against National Curriculum requirements and that standards pupils were achieving were poor, below national expectations and the pupils' capabilities.

Aim

The aim is to ensure that all children receive their curriculum entitlement in design and technology and the standards of their learning of design and technology improve against teacher assessments and assessment tasks.

Success criteria

1   Teachers' medium term planning will incorporate teaching activities designed to enable children to learn the ideas, skills, knowledge and attitudes described in the National Curriculum Programmes of Study for design and technology;

2   Where possible, DT activities and learning will be appropriately related to other subjects;

3   The resources necessary for the children to effectively carry out and learn from the DT activities will be in place;

4   Classroom organisation and teaching methods will support the achievement of criteria 1–3 above.

5   As a result of the planned teaching and learning activities, teachers will be able to accurately assess their children's attainments in DT against the criteria of the National Curriculum;

6   A simple record system of DT attainments will be in place for each child and teachers will begin to use them.

7   An evaluation exercise will confirm that the above criteria have been achieved and that the planned activities are taking place;

8   There will be an agreed time-table for further evaluation and review of the plan.

Example 2 — Key issue

Develop Information Technology provision to meet National Curriculum standards

Suggestion

Activity 17
This, the second example, although a better example of an action plan designed to meet a key issue identified in an OFSTED inspection report, does not satisfy the criteria specified earlier in this chapter. How could this be improved?

Tasks:

- purchase suitable hardware and software in order to raise standards in IT;
- develop staff expertise in teaching and assessing children's IT capability through in-service training;
- develop curriculum planning to include more specific references to how and where IT will be used;
- keep governing body informed of all developments.

Personnel:

- IT coordinator to work with all subject coordinators on planning opportunities and applications for IT.

Resources budget:

- purchase of a further A7000 computer for Key Stage 1: £1200;
- purchase of software relevant to subjects £400;
- training packages for all staff: £800.

Monitoring:

- HT and IT coordinator will carry out classroom observation and discussion with children to assess standards and progress.

Success Criteria:

- standards in all National Curriculum IT Programmes of Study rising as measured by teacher assessment.

Bibliography

BASTIDE, D. (1998) *Coordinating religious education across the primary school* (London: Falmer Press).

BELL, D. (1992) 'Coordinating Science in Primary Schools: a role model?' *Evaluation and Research in Education*, **6**, 2–3, pp. 155–171.

BIRCH, J. (1995) 'Coordinating English at Key Stage 1' in DAVIES, J. (ed) *Developing a Leadership Role in the Key Stage 1 Curriculum* (London: Falmer Press).

BIRCH, T. (1995) 'Developing the role of the Key Stage 1 IT coordinator: A case of the hare or the tortoise' in DAVIES, J. (ed) *Developing a Leadership Role in the Key Stage 1 Curriculum* (London: Falmer Press).

BLEASE, D. and LEVER, D. (1992) 'What do primary headteachers really do?', *Educational Studies*, **8**, 2.

BOEKESTEIN, D. (1995) 'Tackling technology in the early years' in DAVIES, J. (ed) *Developing a Leadership Role in the Key Stage 1 Curriculum* (London: Falmer Press).

BOWE, K. (1995) 'The new science coordinator' in DAVIES, J. (ed) *Developing a Leadership Role in the Key Stage 1 Curriculum* (London: Falmer Press).

BOWRING-CARR, C. and WEST-BURNHAM, J. (1997) *Effective Learning in Schools* (London: Pitman).

BOYLE, B. (1995) 'Providing a sense of direction in Key Stage 2' in HARRISON, M. (ed) *Developing a Leadership Role in the Key Stage 2 Curriculum* (London: Falmer Press).

BROWN, T. (1998) 'Coordinating mathematics across the primary school', in HARRISON, M. (ed) *Developing a Leadership Role in the Key Stage 2 Curriculum* (London: Falmer Press).

BRYSON, B. (1989) *The Lost Continent* (London: Minerva).

CAMPBELL, R. J. (1985) *Developing the Primary School Curriculum* (London: Holt Saunders).

CAMPBELL, R. J. and NEILL, S. R. (1994) *Primary Teachers at Work* (London: Routledge).

CHEDZOY, S. (1995) 'Developing a leadership role at Key Stage 1 — Physical Education' in DAVIES, J. (ed) *Developing a Leadership Role in the Key Stage 1 Curriculum* (London: Falmer Press).

CLEMSON, D. (1996) 'Information Technology in the National Curriculum' in COULBY, D. and WARD, S. (eds) *The Primary Core National Curriculum: Policy into Practice* (London: Cassell).

COCKCROFT, W. H. (1982) *Mathematics Counts* (London: HMSO).

CROSS, A. (1995) 'Design and Technology at Key Stage 2' in HARRISON, M. (ed) *Developing a Leadership Role in the Key Stage 2 Curriculum* (London: Falmer Press).

CROSS, A. (1998) *Coordinating design and technology across the primary school* (London: Falmer Press).

CROSS, A. and BYRNE, D. (1995) 'Coordinating science at Key Stage 2' in HARRISON, M. (ed) *Developing a Leadership Role in the Key Stage 2 Curriculum* (London: Falmer Press).

CROSS, A. and CROSS, S. (1993) 'Running a professional development day in your school', in HARRISON, M. (ed) *Beyond the Core Curriculum* (Plymouth: Northcote House).

DADDS, M. (1997) 'School improvement inside out', *Education 3–13*, **25**, 3, pp. 3–9.

DAVIES, J. (1995a) 'The history coordinator at Key Stage 1' in DAVIES, J. (ed) *Developing a Leadership Role in the Key Stage 1 Curriculum* (London: Falmer Press).

DAVIES, J. (1995b) 'The history coordinator in Key Stage 2' in HARRISON, M. (ed) *Developing a Leadership Role in the Key Stage 2 Curriculum* (London: Falmer Press).

DAVIES, J. and REDMOND, J. (1998) *Coordinating history across the primary school* (London: Falmer Press).

DEAN, J. (1987) *Managing the Primary School* (Kent: Croome Helm).

DES (1978) *Primary Education in England: A Survey by HM Inspectors of Schools* (London: HMSO).

DES (1991) *Developing School Management — Report by the School Management Task Force* (London: HMSO).

DfEE (1997) *From Targets into Action: Guidance to Support Effective Target-setting in Schools* (London: HMSO).

DfEE\OFSTED (1996) *Setting Targets to Raise Standards: A Survey of Good Practice* (London: HMSO).

DfEE/QCA (1998) *1997 Benchmarking Information for Key Stages 1 and 2* (London: QCA).

DRUCKER, D. F. (1967) *The Effective Executive* (London: Heinemann).

DUNHAM, J. (1995) *Developing Effective Management* (London: Heinemann).

EVERARD, K. B. and MORRIS, G. (1985) *Effective School Management* (London: PCP).

GALTON, M. (1995) *Crisis in the Primary Classroom* (London: David Fulton).

GREENWOOD, M. and GAUNT, H. (1994) *Total Quality Management for Schools* (London: Cassell).

HALL, V. (1996) *Dancing on the Ceiling* (London: Paul Chapman).

HARRISON, M. (1995a) 'Working towards becoming the mathematics coordinator', in HARRISON, M. (ed) *Developing a Leadership Role in the Key Stage 2 Curriculum* (London: Falmer Press).

HARRISON, M. (1995b) 'Getting IT together in Key Stage 2' in HARRISON, M. (ed) *Developing a Leadership Role in the Key Stage 2 Curriculum* (London: Falmer Press).

HARRISON, M. (1995) 'Developing a Key Stage 2 policy for your subject' in HARRISON, M. (ed) *Developing a Leadership Role in the Key Stage 2 Curriculum* (London: Falmer Press).

HARRISON, M. (1998) *Coordinating ICT across the primary school* (London: Falmer Press).

HARRISON, M. A. and GILL, S. C. (1992) *Primary School Management* (London: Heinemann).

HARRISON, S. and THEAKER, K. (1989) *Curriculum Leadership and Coordination in the Primary School* (Whalley: Guild House Press).

HENNESSY, S. (1998) *Coordinating music across the primary school* (London: Falmer Press).

HODGKINSON, C. (1991) *Educational Leadership* (New York: Suny).

HOLLY, P. and SOUTHWORTH, G. (1989) *The Developing School* (London: Falmer Press).

HOLMES, G. (1993) *Essential School Leadership* (London: Kogan Page).

HOLOCHA, J. (1998) *Coordinating geography across the primary school* (London: Falmer Press).

HUSTLER, D. and STONE, V. (1996) 'Lay inspectors' in OUSTON, J., EARLEY, P. and FIDLER, B. (eds) *OFSTED Inspections: The Early Experience* (London: David Fulton).

KELLY, M. (1995) 'Action first — thinking later!' *Management in Education*, **9**, 2.

KYDD, L., CRAWFORD, M. and RICHES, C. (1997) *Professional Development for Educational Management* (Buckingham: Open University).

LAAR, B. (1998) 'Beat the inspector', *TES Primary*, 3 March 1998.

MATTOCK, G. (1995) 'Religious education in Key Stage 2' in HARRISON, M. (ed) *Developing a Leadership Role in the Key Stage 2 Curriculum* (London: Falmer Press).

MATTOCK, G. and PRESTON, G. (1995) 'The religious education coordinator in the early years' in DAVIES, J. (ed) *Developing a Leadership Role in the Key Stage 1 Curriculum* (London: Falmer Press).

MORTIMORE, P., SAMMONS, P., STOLL, L., LEWIS, D. and ECOB, R. (1988) *School Matters* (Open Books: Froome).

NEWTON, L. and NEWTON, D. (1998) *Coordinating science across the primary school* (London: Falmer Press).

NNP (1998) *National Numeracy Project — Numeracy Lessons* (London: Beam mathematics).

OFSTED (1994a) *Primary matters: A discussion on teaching and learning in primary schools* (London: HMSO).

OFSTED (1994b) *OFSTED Framework for Inspection* (London: HMSO).

OFSTED (1995) *Guidance on the Inspection of Nursery and Primary Schools* (London: HMSO).

OFSTED (1995b) *Planning Improvement: School's Post-inspection Action Plans* (London: HMSO).

OFSTED (1997a) *Inspection and Re-inspection of Schools from September 1997: New Requirements and Guidance on their Implementation* (London: HMSO).

OFSTED (1997b) *The Teaching of Number in Three Inner-urban LEAs* (London: HMSO).

OFSTED (1998) *School Evaluation Matters* (London: HMSO).

PAISLEY, A. and PAISLEY, A. (1989) *Effective Management in Primary Schools* (Basil Blackwell: Oxford).

PAY, F. (1998) 'Accepting the blame', *Managing Schools Today*, **7**, 5.

PIOTROWSKI, J. (1995) 'Coordinating the art curriculum in Key Stage 2' in HARRISON, M. (ed) *Developing a Leadership Role in the Key Stage 2 Curriculum* (London: Falmer Press).

PIOTROWSKI, J., CLEMENTS, R. and ROBERTS, I. (1998) *Coordinating art across the primary school* (London: Falmer Press).

PLAYFOOT, D., SKELTON, M. and SOUTHWORTH, G. (1989) *The Primary School Management Book* (London: Mary Glasgow Publishers Limited).

POLLARD, A. (1985) *The Social World of the Primary School* (London: Cassell).

RAY, R. (1995a) 'Not Sunflowers again! Coordinating art at Key Stage 1' in DAVIES, K. (ed) *Developing a Leadership Role in the Key Stage 1 Curriculum* (London: Falmer Press).

RAY, R. (1995b) 'Reading the changes' in HARRISON, M. (ed) *Developing a Leadership Role in the Key Stage 2 Curriculum* (London: Falmer Press).

RAY, R. (1995c) 'Reading at Key Stage 1' in DAVIES, J. (ed) *Developing a Leadership Role in the Key Stage 1 Curriculum* (London: Falmer Press).

RICHARDS, C. (1995) 'Curriculum leadership: Challenges for headteachers', *Education 3–13*, **23**, 3, pp. 3–10.

RAYMOND, C. (1998) *Coordinating physical education across the primary school* (London: Falmer Press).

ROBERTS, G. R. (1995) 'Writing' in HARRISON, M. (ed) *Developing a Leadership Role in the Key Stage 2 Curriculum* (London: Falmer Press).

RODGER, R. (1995) 'Geography in the early years: The role of the subject manager' in DAVIES, J. (ed) *Developing a Leadership Role in the Key Stage 1 Curriculum* (London: Falmer Press).

SANDERSON, P. (1995) 'Physical education and dance: Leading the way' in HARRISON, M. (ed) *Developing a Leadership Role in the Key Stage 2 Curriculum* (London: Falmer Press).

SCAA (1995a) *Consistency in Teacher Assessment: Exemplification of Standards, Science* (London: SCAA).

SCAA (1995b) *Consistency in Teacher Assessment: Exemplification of Standards, Mathematics* (London: SCAA).

SCAA (1995c) *Consistency in Teacher Assessment: Exemplification of Standards, English* (London: SCAA).

SCAA (1997a) *Expectations in Information Technology* (London: SCAA).

SCAA (1997b) *Expectations in Design and Technology* (London: SCAA).

SCAA (1997c) *Expectations in Physical Education* (London: SCAA).

SCAA (1997d) *Expectations in Art* (London: SCAA).

SCAA (1997e) *Expectations in Music* (London: SCAA).

SCAA (1997f) *Expectations in History* (London: SCAA).

SCAA (1997g) *Expectations in Geography* (London: SCAA).

SCHRAG, E., NELSON and SIMINOWSKY, T. (1985) 'Helping employees cope with change' *Childcare Information Exchange*, September.

SERGIOVANNI, T. J. (1996) *Leadership for the Schoolhouse* (San Francisco: Jossey-Bass).

STEWART, B. and HOCKING, I. (1995) 'Directions in mathematics: The coordinator effect' in DAVIES, J. (ed) *Developing a Leadership Role in the Key Stage 1 Curriculum* (London: Falmer Press).

SUTTON, R. (1991) *Assessment: A Framework for Teaching* (Windsor: NFER–NELSON).

SUTTON, R. (1995) *Assessment for Learning* (Salford: RS Publications).

TAGG, B. (1996) 'The school in an information age' in TAGG, B. (ed) *Developing a whole-school IT Policy* (London: Pitman).

THE NATIONAL COMMISSION ON EDUCATION (1993) *Learning to Succeed: A Radical Look at Education Today and a Strategy for the Future* (London: Heinemann).

TRESSELL, R. (1905) *The Ragged Trousered Philanthropists* (London: Paladin).

TTA (1997) *National Standards for Subject Leaders — Revised Draft July 1997* (London: TTA).

WALKER, A. (1995) 'Sounding the right note' in HARRISON, M. (ed) *Developing a Leadership Role in the Key Stage 2 Curriculum* (London: Falmer Press).

WALKER, R. (1995) 'Starting off on the right note' in DAVIES, J. (ed) *Developing a Leadership Role in the Key Stage 1 Curriculum* (London: Falmer Press).

WALTERS, M. and MARTIN, T. (1998a) *Coordinating English at Key Stage 1* (London: Falmer Press).

WALTERS, M. and MARTIN, T. (1998b) *Coordinating English at Key Stage 2* (London: Falmer Press).

WEINER, G. (1985) *Just a Bunch of Girls* (Milton Keynes: OUP).

WEST, N. (1995) *Middle Management in the Primary School: A Development Guide for Curriculum Leaders, Subject Managers and Senior Staff* (London: David Fulton).

WEST-BURNHAM, J. (1997) *Managing Quality in Schools* (London: Pitman).

WHITAKER, P. (1983) *The Primary Head* (London: Heinemann).

WHITAKER, P. (1997) *Primary Schools and the Future: Celebration, Challenges and Choices* (Buckingham: Open University).

Index

ORDER FORM

Post: *Customer Services Department, Falmer Press, Rankine Road, Basingstoke, Hampshire, RG24 8PR*
Tel: *(01256) 813000* Fax: *(01256) 479438*
E-mail: *book.orders@tandf.co.uk*

10% DISCOUNT AND FREE P&P FOR SCHOOLS OR INDIVIDUALS ORDERING THE COMPLETE SET ORDER YOUR SET NOW. WITH CREDIT CARD PAYMENTS, YOU WON'T BE CHARGED TILL DESPATCH.

TITLE	DUE	ISBN	PRICE	QTY
SUBJECT LEADERS' HANDBOOKS SET		**(RRP £207.20)**	**£185.00**	
Coordinating Science	2/98	0 7507 0688 0	£12.95	
Coordinating Design and Technology	2/98	0 7507 0689 9	£12.95	
Coordinating Maths	2/98	0 7507 0687 2	£12.95	
Coordinating Physical Education	2/98	0 7507 0693 7	£12.95	
Coordinating History	2/98	0 7507 0691 0	£12.95	
Coordinating Music	2/98	0 7507 0694 5	£12.95	
Coordinating Geography	2/98	0 7507 0692 9	£12.95	
Coordinating English at Key Stage 1	4/98	0 7507 0685 6	£12.95	
Coordinating English at Key Stage 2	4/98	0 7507 0686 4	£12.95	
Coordinating IT	4/98	0 7507 0690 2	£12.95	
Coordinating Art	4/98	0 7507 0695 3	£12.95	
Coordinating Religious Education	Late 98	0 7507 0613 9	£12.95	
Management Skills for SEN Coordinators	Late 98	0 7507 0697 X	£12.95	
Building a Whole School Assessment Policy	Late 98	0 7507 0698 8	£12.95	
Curriculum Coordinator and OFSTED Inspection	Late 98	0 7507 0699 6	£12.95	
Coordinating Curriculum in Smaller Primary School	Late 98	0 7507 0700 3	£12.95	

Value of Books	
P&P*	
Total	

I wish to pay by:

*Please add p&p
orders up to £25   *10%*
orders from £25 to £50   *5%*
orders over £50   *free*

❑ Cheque *(Pay Falmer Press)*
❑ Pro-forma invoice
❑ Credit Card *(Mastercard / Visa / AmEx)*

Card Number _____ *Expiry Date* _____

Signature _____

Name _____ *Title/Position* _____

School _____

Address _____

_____

Postcode _____ *Country* _____

Tel no. _____ *Fax* _____

E-mail _____

Ref: 1197BFSLAD

All prices are correct at time of going to print but may change without notice